Brief Homage to Pluto and Other Poems

The Lockert Library of Poetry in Translation

Series Editors
Peter Cole, Richard Sieburth, and Rosanna Warren
Series Editor Emeritus (1991–2016)
Richard Howard

For other titles in the Lockert Library, see the list at the end of this volume.

BRIEF HOMAGE TO PLUTO

AND OTHER POEMS

FABIO PUSTERLA

Selected and Translated by
WILL SCHUTT

Princeton University Press
Princeton and Oxford

Published by Princeton University Press
41 William Street, Princeton, New Jersey 08540
99 Banbury Road, Oxford OX2 6JX

press.princeton.edu

All Rights Reserved

Library of Congress Cataloging-in-Publication Data

Names: Pusterla, Fabio, 1957–author. | Schutt, Will, 1981–translator.
Title: Brief homage to Pluto and other poems / Fabio Pusterla;
   selected and translated by Will Schutt.
Description: Princeton: Princeton University Press, 2023. | Series: The Lockert Library of
   poetry in translation | Includes bibliographical references.
Identifiers: LCCN 2022019125 (print) | LCCN 2022019126 (ebook) | ISBN 9780691245096
   (paperback) | ISBN 9780691245102 (hardback) | ISBN 9780691245119 (ebook)
Subjects: LCSH: Pusterla, Fabio, 1957—Translations into English. | LCGFT: Poetry.
Classification: LCC PQ4876.U82 B75 2023 (print) | LCC PQ4876.U82 (ebook) |
   DDC 851/.914—dc23/eng/20220426
LC record available at https://lccn.loc.gov/2022019125
LC ebook record available at https://lccn.loc.gov/2022019126

British Library Cataloging-in-Publication Data is available

Editorial: Anne Savarese and James Collier
Production Editorial: Theresa Liu
Text and Jacket/Cover Design: Pamela L. Schnitter
Production: Lauren Reese
Publicity: Alyssa Sanford and Carmen Jimenez
Copyeditor: Jodi Beder

Cover images: Topographic map by Rainer Lesniewski / Shutterstock. Tree illustration from the series, "The trees are burning in your promised land," coal on paper, cm 150 x 200, 2016. Illustration © Luca Mengoni.

The Lockert Library of Poetry in Translation is supported by a bequest from Charles Lacy Lockert (1888–1974)

This book has been composed in Minion Pro and Avenir

10 9 8 7 6 5 4 3 2 1

Contents

Translator's Introduction

One of the first things I learned about Fabio Pusterla was that he had a strong distaste for the label Swiss Italian, *schweizer italienisch*. The term attaches itself to the work in review after review, and he's frequently asked its implications. The possible implications of the poet's origins probably ought to be examined, especially because it is unfamiliar ground to most English-speaking readers, but then these origins should be moved on from, points of departure, as they so often are treated in his poems. I am reminded of Eugenio Montale, another Italian poet who presses reality into the service of the imagination, once remarking, "I always begin with the real."

The real, then: Pusterla was born in Mendrisio, Switzerland, in 1957, and continues to live between Como and Lugano, where he teaches literature at a Swiss high school and the University of Italian Switzerland. He grew up with one foot in the province of Como and the rest of his body in the Italian-speaking part of Switzerland, the son of an Italian watchmaker raised on the Swiss side of the border and a Swiss homemaker raised on the Italian side, a boy who first encountered "serious" books on a spinning rack at his neighborhood supermarket, a boy literary not by birth but by choice—though his paternal grandfather, a barber, penned the occasional poem and saddled his son, Pusterla's father, with the name Elios Virgilio. When he read *Dubliners*, as a teenager in the 1960s, Pusterla "understood that Chiasso (the Swiss town where he came of age) was in Ireland, though no one seemed to know it, because its odors and the fabric and metal of its days and the color of its nights and the sound of its trains seemed identical to those [he] was discovering" in Joyce's book. In-betweenness, then, a condition of those born on a border and those, no matter how geographically rooted, who gravitate to books and spend the rest of their lives negotiating between the acute renderings of the imagination and the foggy realms of the actual. Chiasso, as Pusterla describes it, was "a backwater with an economy that ran on gas, watches, and cigarettes, on contraband and freight traffic, dominated by the checkpoint and the railroad, politically blinkered, culturally set in its ways." In books he found "other realities that were more real than the reality of others."[1]

Pusterla seems, at times, equal parts homebound and boundless. He lives with his wife Claudia on the bottom two railroad-style floors of a house that belonged to his grandparents (his sister occupies the top half), yet the library in their living room is arranged like a world map: by country, multilingual. Though one detects in his work echoes of other native sons and daughters of northern Italy, like Montale, and of the Italian-speaking part of Switzerland, like Giorgio Orelli and Vittorio Sereni, Pusterla is just as quick to mention the influence of farther-flung writers like Dostoevsky, Dylan Thomas, and Cormac McCarthy. On the one hand, he is *the* Italian translator of a fellow Swiss, the francophone poet Philippe Jaccottet. On the other, he is, well, a translator, one who must cross linguistic borders, and he has lived through, in Michael Hofmann's words, the trauma of bilingualism—or trilingualism, counting dialects. He writes in standard Italian but some of his poetry titles come from dialect words, like 1999's *Pietra sangue,* in dialect *piétra saanch,* the name of one of seven types of stone applied in the Como region to scagliola, or "poor man's marble," a kind of inlay for architectural

[1] Fabio Pusterla, "When Chiasso Was in Ireland," in *Quando Chiasso era in Irlanda* (Edizioni Casagrande, 2012).

elements and sculptures. Or 2014's *Argéman*, which refers to bands of snow or ice that perennially cover hard-to-access mountain passes. *Argéman* also means avalanche.

Flinty landscapes are typical of his work. Ditto the withdrawn lyric "I." The "I" and "eye" of the poems often scan for language in a negative space, an alpine "labyrinth" "of piss and lumber" that has a post-industrial, post-human feel. Post, because Pusterla *qua* nature poet is equally interested in (I almost want to say accepting of) the human-made, with both boots in the Anthropocene, an age when, even in the nine villages of the Valsolda (pop. 1,400 or so), town and country can no longer be "considered independently: foxes and spores wander megalopolises, fine dust particles fall invisibly from the clearest skies." In-betweenness, again: Pusterla is drawn to the natural spectacles of the world when they "appear on a border or a rift zone: when their presence is situated on the visible edge of the presence or absence of humankind, creating a kind of intermediary zone, a disquieting or interstitial zone, in which 'nature' cannot fully be itself, and human presence/absence seems to reach a limit, a point of collapse."[2]

The effect of Pusterla's poems may best be captured by his own prose. This passage, from an essay on walking, conveys the expansive, drifty quality of much of the more recent work that I have chosen to translate, poems that accommodate rugged landscapes, metaphysical musings, a copse of trees, a running river, snatches of overheard conversation, and, for good measure, a memory jarred loose:

Sometimes, in a vast, secluded, almost hostile landscape, far from home, in foreign countries with mysterious languages,

[2] Stefano Modeo, "Poesia e ecologia. Conversazioni con Fabio Pusterla" (Nazione Indiana, 2020).

those of us who are lost will stumble upon short stretches of familiar, unexpectedly hospitable land: a clearing, a stand of acacia trees, long rows of crops, something about the farmland or houses, the smell of tar. The detail takes us back to experience, to the blurry memory of something: a place we know by touch, a step our foot instinctively, naturally gives its weight to, a name we recognize and which, for a moment, puts us at ease. What is it if not a sense of self? The recognition of another path we walked a long time ago, a path paved inside us, the warmth of a faint memory reemerging? This, I tell myself, is what is meant by a mother tongue: a place we feel at home, the rhythm of words that have always belonged to us, the color of sounds and syllables. Not meanings, which change. Not elegance or logic, but rhythm, the pulse of language, whatever makes us veer to the left, the smell of the earth where we come to rest, the circulation of blood and flow of water. People with a destination in mind use language to forge ahead and rush down the streets of syntax. People without a destination, on the other hand, reside inside the language, wander through the language as if it were a sweeping plain or dark forest, stuttering. And when they veer left, they don't quite retrace their steps; sometimes they find, in their lostness, a memory of themselves inscribed in the language, strange symbols on the bark of trees, signals; the awareness of their own being and of their not being there but forever somewhere else. Not there or in any place, and yet in all places equally, because being inside language may simply mean walking, joining up with others and parting ways down the road, carrying with you voices, fragments of stories, images.[3]

[3] Pusterla, "Ambulando Solvitur," in *Quando Chiasso era in Irlanda* (Edizioni Casagrande, 2012).

Wandering things, Pusterla's poems are loose and less purposive than other forms of speech, language with the GPS switched off. Disequipped for the requirements of life, as John Ashbery has it. Rhymes appear irregularly and enjambment frequently; meters are mixed (many poems intermingle hendecasyllable lines and *settenari*). Now and again the poems slip the bonds of punctuation. In such *terrain vague* the emotional sources of the work can be hard to pin down. Tenderness and mordancy abut. The poems wonder aloud how the landscape might speak "of other things, of us," not describing the external world so much as groping for a verbal equivalent of interior experience. They inhabit, in short, a nebulous realm. The Italian word *nebbia*, meaning mist, fog, cloud, is the title of one of his longer prose poems, a word that conditions the poem's form(lessness):

> I'm doing, you see, what I usually prohibit myself from doing: writing freely, following no logic, letting the words emerge on their own, almost free, almost beyond my control.
>
> Dangerous game, vain maybe, which the fog itself, occluding things, invites me to play. A way of summoning what is absent, or, more likely, of deceiving oneself.
>
> —"FOG"

This wayfaring attitude toward language approaches *ars poetica* status in the poem "To Those to Come":

> meaning you, who'll turn back
> and look at us from the peaks
> of your brilliant age, like one who scans a valley
> he can't recall having crossed:
> you won't see us behind the screen of fog.
> But we were here, ministering to the voice.

Not every day, not every hour
of the day, only from time to time,
when mustering a little strength
appeared possible.
We'd close the door
behind us, leaving behind
our sumptuous homes,
and, picking up the path again, drift on.

The correlation between writing and walking is even more explicit in the injunction that closes the poem "Thirty Years On": "Walk, write." The Italian is better: *Cammini, scrivi,* with the bounce of those four long *i*'s (*ca-mee-nee, scree-vee*) and the inevitable echo of Dante's *Divine Comedy* (*nel mezzo del* cammin *di nostra vita*) and, less expected, Machado's caminante *no hay* camino: "walk" as verb and noun. When I visited him in Albogasio, in January 2020, weeks before the first reported case of Covid-19 in Lombardy, Pusterla took me to see one of the neighboring villages, built about halfway up the mountain above Lake Lugano. Fabio is, I should preface, a gracious correspondent and an unstinting host, like many Italians (a do-unto-others attitude I've always attributed to the fact that the Italian word *ospite* means both guest and host). As we floated about and our conversation turned friendlier, freer, we soon found ourselves facing a forest trail at the back end of the town. One habitat ended and another began. I stopped and watched Fabio, as if propelled, pick up the pace, dropping everything—guest, dinner plans, the thread of the conversation—and march off into the woods. Eventually he turned back around, smiling broadly, but I couldn't help wishing I'd not been in the way.

To call Pusterla a nature poet is to limit him. He does nature *and* people, his work invested as much in voice as it is in image. In

"Testimonies," all that stands is speech. A braid of voices comments on the murder of an immigrant mother, a victim of domestic abuse who had pinned her hopes on Switzerland. While the onlookers and neighbors offer a mix of empty handouts ("One time I bought her a coffee / after she broke down / in the street") and callous shrugs ("She must have had her reasons for filing a complaint"), the central figure slips through the sieve of the poem.

Despite eight books of critically acclaimed poetry under his belt, several major awards, a healthy national reputation, a documentary dedicated to his life that manages to capture—for once!—the messy organic process of making a poem, and an impressive array of translators who have published English versions of individual poems (Damiano Abeni and Moira Egan, Geoffrey Brock, Chad Davidson) and a book-length selection of his first six volumes by the British translator Simon Knight, Pusterla remains a reluctant poet, describing himself in one poem as "making do in the kitchen / writing poems, not being a poet." Reading *When Chiasso Was in Ireland* and *Arnold's Nerve*, two collections of his occasional prose—reviews, talks, memoirs, essays—I was struck by how many begin with ambivalence, hesitation, the subjunctive mood. For Pusterla, the coteries that dominated the Italian literary scene in the 1960s and '70s, each with particular claims for art and culture, and each with its own political or regional affiliation, are unviable; unsuited to this day and age, perhaps. Pusterla is acutely aware of the marginal place poetry has occupied in Italy since about 1975, the year Montale picked up the Nobel Prize and Pasolini was crushed under a car on a beach in Ostia.

That is not to accuse him of being a wishy-washy or aloof poet, chanting sonnets in his convent's narrow rooms. If anything, the poet chafes at the trammeled interiority of life. "Hell is," he writes, "not being others." Instead, Pusterla has built an admirable career and life left of center, one I am tempted to call heroic in a low-key, act-local, twenty-first-century way, publishing with small presses, teaching at a high school, fostering emerging or under-recognized poets as the editor of the Ali poetry imprint. His first book, *Concessione all'inverno* (Concession to Winter), came out in 1985, when he was twenty-eight, with Edizioni Casagrande, an independent press based in Canton Ticino, and since then he has elected to publish almost all of his subsequent work—eight more books of poetry, various translations, essays, introductions—with Casagrande or Marcos y Marcos, another independent press based in Milan, though surely he could have plumped for a bigger publisher. Off-to-the-sideness seems part and parcel of his poetic enterprise and his understanding of contemporary poetry as a distant suburb of the seat of culture: "Perhaps the marginal status of contemporary poetry, the fact that it has no perch on the market, that it dangles on the edge of the semiosphere, that it is, in short, vulnerable, can prompt, may already have prompted, a new and different dialogue that begins from the bottom, from the margins, from outside."[4]

Centerlessness, diffuseness, marginality—for Pusterla these qualities can spill into more overt political themes at a time when anti-immigrant sentiments and replacement theories have surged in Europe, particularly in Pusterla's backyard. Northern Italy is home to the populist Northern League Party, founded in the 1990s and currently helmed by Matteo Salvini; picture a paler Trump. Now known simply as the Lega, the party is associated with nativist, Eurosceptic, and libertarian platforms. To give you just one small example of the Lega's absurdly ahistorical fearmongering: their advertising campaigns include a poster depicting a Native American chief, warbonnet and all, with a caption underneath that reads "They

[4] Pusterla, "Domande, margini, rive," in *Il Nervo di Arnold* (Marcos y Marcos, 2007).

Let Foreigners In . . . Now They Live on Reservations." A member of a similar party in Switzerland, the regionalist, right-wing Ticino League, is lampooned in "Dragonfly," the long poem at the end of this selection, as is the moral indifference of the European elite in another long poem, "April 2016: Postcards from Italy," a poem I love but which seems to me too culturally insular for American readers. Hence I am smuggling the end of the poem into this note:

> Who is this guy smoking next to me,
> sucking on a cigar and chewing the fat?
> He smiles in the flickering morning light, cops a look
> at the rooftops, women passing by, clouds,
> then furtively folds up the paper, lifts his eyes
> and sets off after his wife with the air of someone
> who has won again, who always knows
> he's won, and won what now?
>
> He's who he is, maybe I'm me, nobody's us.

As a translator I have been lucky to have Fabio's helpful explanations of allusions or difficult passages, to have been provided context for particular poems. Because Fabio himself is an accomplished translator—the foremost Italian translator and exponent of Philippe Jaccottet—he knows that translation is a process of give and take, of fidelity and improvisation, and has written convincingly, as I see it, about the demands placed on a translator to put in right relation creative resourcefulness and critical analysis, to ferry across the meaning and the music of a poem. I think Fabio would agree that, in poetic translation, the ear has it.

Attention to the dominant sounds has guided many of my translation choices. I have tried to bring across the sense I have when reading Pusterla of controlled variety, each line tied to the previous line yet also making its own distinct effect; to preserve the shifting tones, now hushed, now keening, and the prevailing consonant and vowel sounds, though of course not always in the same lines or even stanzas.

Take for example "Ermanno's Breath," "Il Respiro di Ermanno," a brief, perfectly understated elegy. Here is the Italian:

Caro Ermanno, ho ascoltato
un poeta polacco di nome Jaroslaw Mikolajewski
leggere una poesia che parlava del fiato,
del respiro del padre scomparso trovato in cantina
con stupore, dentro un materassino gonfiabile
di trent'anni prima.

Il fiato, pensa, la cosa più fragile, resta
di un uomo talvolta, nei luoghi più strani, e nel fiato
galleggiano forse miriadi di quei moscerini
che ti parevano lieti, o altre forme disperse

come piccoli punti di voce.

Anche tu ci hai lasciato un respiro,
Ermanno, un respiro e dei versi.

And here is my English version:

Dear Ermanno, I heard
a Polish poet named Jarosław Mikołajewski
read a poem that spoke of breath,
about the shock of finding his dead father's breath
in an inflatable mattress in the basement
from thirty years before.

Breath, think about it, sometimes the wispiest part of
a man lingers in the strangest places, and in that breath

maybe there floats a multitude of those gnats
you thought looked glad, or other dispersed shapes

like pinpricks of a voice.

You too left us a breath,
Ermanno, a breath and some verse.

The original poem is dominated by *o*'s and *p*'s, both found in the Italian words for breath, *respiro,* and poetry, *poesia.* The *o*'s in the beginning—*Caro Ermanno ho ascoltato*—immediately prepare us for this meditation on breath and accompany us for the rest of the poem (*poeta polacco* to *fiato* to *uomo* to *voce*). *P* carries the memory of *padre* (father) all the way to *piccoli punti* (little points), reminding us of the emotional center of the poem, which turns from mourning the dead father to honoring Ermanno Krumm, a poet who died young having left behind a single book of poetry, called *Breath.* The tone by the end is not dirgelike but full of wonderment at what lives on, its *piccoli punti* of voice not unlike the uncut hair of graves.

To convey the poem's truth-telling music, in David Ferry's inspired phrase, I have kept those *p*'s ("wispiest" not "fragile"; "dispersed" not "scattered"; "pinpricks" not "little points") and the double *m*'s in stanza 2 that signal the shift to addressing Krumm (*forse un* m*iriadi di quei* m*oscerini* becomes *m*aybe a *m*ultitude of those gnats). To communicate the air of regularity and measure in the original, I have made the English lines largely iambic, though the number of feet fluctuates: — READ a POEM that SPOKE of BREATH, from THIRty YEARS beFORE, and so on. That *voice* and *verse* share the same sounds as *voce e versi* is one of those instances of dumb luck in the translation business that I'll take, though one can easily imagine another translator opting for a lower or domesticating register, "some poems," say, or even "some lines."

The poems included in my selection come from Pusterla's six most recent books of poetry: *Le cose senza storia* (Things with No History), *Folla sommersa* (Buried Crowd), *Pietra sangue, Corpo stellare* (Stellar Body), *Argéman*, and *Cenere, o terra* (Ashes, or Earth). These are the books and poems I have lived with longest, the first blush. I initially read Pusterla's books in reverse chronological order, or almost, starting with *Argéman* (2014) and *Corpo stellare* (2010), long shapely collections that both top two hundred pages. His most recent book, *Cenere, o terra*, another two hundred pages, appeared at the end of 2018, several years after I had begun translating him.

It is as an editor that I have meddled most. Within each section, the poems have been arranged not in chronological order but in such a way as to give readers the sense of a continuous, tonally consistent work. I have been drawn to the shadowy aspect of Pusterla's poetics, his elegiac moods and haunted landscapes. (The Pluto of the title is the Roman god of the underworld, not the planet.) My selection represents a small fraction of Pusterla's work, but one I believe serves as a good introduction and conveys what an ambitious, imaginative, humane, and worldly poet Pusterla is.

Poems 1994–2004

A quelli che verranno

Allora voi, che volgerete
lo sguardo verso di noi dalle vette
dei vostri tempi splendidi, come chi scruta una valle
che non ricorda neppure di avere percorsa:
non ci vedrete, dietro lo schermo di nebbie.
Ma eravamo qui, a custodire la voce.
Non ogni giorno e non in ogni ora
del giorno; qualche volta, soltanto,
quando sembrava possibile
raccogliere un po' di forza.
Ci chiudevamo la porta
dietro le spalle, abbandonando
le nostre case sontuose
e riprendevamo il cammino, senza meta.

To Those to Come

meaning you, who'll turn back
and look at us from the peaks
of your brilliant age, like one who scans a valley
he can't recall having crossed:
you won't see us behind the screen of fog.
But we were here, ministering to the voice.
Not every day, not every hour
of the day, only from time to time,
when mustering a little strength
appeared possible.
We'd close the door
behind us, leaving behind
our sumptuous homes,
and, picking up the path again, drift on.

Roggia

Passo di qui, tornando da un lungo viaggio,
come in un cimitero di memorie.
La pozzanghera c'è sempre, anche d'estate,
il fango, la sterrata, i ciuffi d'erba
e d'ortica non cambiano mai. Sassi e sterpaglie
spariranno anche loro, soffocati da una morsa
più forte, di cemento, un giorno o l'altro,
e forse prima ancora dei nostri ricordi,
ma per adesso ci sono, ed è il passaggio
desolato che ho scelto per te. L'ultima casa
aperta al vento e alla luce, una pianura
quasi sempre deserta, non amena,
che percorre lentissima
una roggia. Io fumo, sto sul ponte,
e getto anche per te una sigaretta
nell'acqua scura. È un rito
senza senso, meno anche che un rito:
un'abitudine. Già con mio padre, a volte, sotto i fiori,
e mi domando cosa avrà pensato mia madre
di quel tabacco tombale: spettri, vandali?
O forse ha indovinato e non ne parla
per pudore. Full flavor blend, comunque, una miscela
mediocre, piuttosto grezza, Maryland: la sigaretta
rossa dei muratori, o così dicono. Anche il nome
riporta a sogni lisi e fuori corso: Parisienne,
ragazze che sgambettano su un palco al Moulin Rouge,

Irrigation Channel

Back from a long trip, I drop by
as if my memories were buried here.
Even in summer there's always that puddle;
the mud, the gravel road, the tufts of grass
and nettles—they never change. The stones and scrub
will vanish too, strangled by a firmer
concrete grip, one of these days,
maybe before our forgetting has begun,
but for now they're here, and this desolating landscape
is the one I chose for you. The last house
exposed to the wind and light, a plain
nearly always deserted, mean-looking,
sluggishly traversed
by an irrigation channel. I smoke, I stand on the bridge,
I toss an extra cigarette into the dark
water for you. It's a ritual
signifying nothing, less than a ritual—
a habit. I used to bury them under the flowers with my father
and wonder what my mother must have thought
about that tomb of tobacco. Ghosts? Vandals?
Or maybe she guessed and out of modesty
kept it to herself. In any case, full-flavor blend, a coarse,
mediocre cut from Maryland, a brand of reds
bricklayers smoked, or so they say. Parisiennes;
the name alone conjures shopworn dreams:
girls gamboling on stage at the Moulin Rouge,

le luci di Pigalle, la naftalina di un secolo, BB.
O Jeanne Moreau, col suo volto
vastissimo e profondo: le sarebbe piaciuto
questo tabacco. Oggi però inattesi
dall'argine sono spuntati cinque germani
spaventandomi quasi: sono scesi in acqua regali,
risalendo la poca corrente della roggia, e uno di loro
si è voltato un istante.

the lights in Pigalle, the mothballs of an era, B.B.
Or the soulful, open face
of Jeanne Moreau. She would have liked
this brand. But today out of nowhere
five ducks turned up on the embankment,
almost frightening me, regally slipping into the water,
swimming against the weak current, and one of them
turned a moment to face me.

Movimenti ascensionali: Le scale di Albogasio

Case a strapiombo, asperità minori,
un figlio in testa; e, d'infilata, la breva
che prende il lago a sghimbescio, ingannatrice
si tuffa dalla Forca di San Martino,
costeggia rocce e strada e poi s'infuria
subito dopo Gandria, dove l'acqua s'allarga.
È una sera di turbini, in cui scendo
come in un coro per le scale di un paese,
la mano alla barella, che altalena
e striscia lungo i muri, e ad ogni curva
stacca polvere altrove; ultima scorta
di calce per Erminia, la gentile
signora morta altrove, che ritorna
al suo balcone di minuscoli fiori.
Qui si passa nel buio: facendo presa
sullo scalino più basso con il piede,
per rampe verticali e stretti portici. Giù il lago
adesso non si vede, ma risuona
cupo dentro le darsene, e le barche
gemono nel loro cuore di legno e di catrame.
Qualche porta si schiude: chi s'affaccia
guarda in silenzio la nostra strana processione
che cala goffa agli inferi, alle nere
case del sonno. E tuttavia dal basso
sale qualcosa, un soffio umido e denso;
una mano d'aria o un gonfiore

Up and Down the Steps of Albogasio

Houses on cliffs, minor asperities,
a child in mind; and, crosswise, the *breva*
taking the lake at a slant, a shapeshifter,
sweeping down from Saint Martin's Pass,
hugging the rocks and roads, then gusting
past Gandria, where the water widens.
It is an evening of strong winds when I
descend the village stairs, as if in a chorus,
my hand gripping a stretcher that swings
and grazes the walls and at every turn
scrapes away white dust, a final
coat of lime for Erminia, the kind lady
who died somewhere else and is now
returning to her balcony of tiny flowers.
We pass into the dark, testing each
step down as we negotiate the steep
flight and narrow porticoes. The lake below
drops from sight but we can hear it
darkly lapping at the docks, and the tarred
wooden hearts of boats groaning.
Doors open, faces appear.
They don't say a word as they watch
our strange procession lumber down to the black
houses of sleep. Yet something rises
from the bottom, a thick, moist draft,
a handful or swelling of air

s'insinua e chiede ascolto,
vita remota che risale dall'acqua, ancora informe
eppure già presente, già imperiosa
nel suo esistere scarno:
che incrocia noi in discesa e va più in alto,
come fumo sottile. Antiche scale
le scale di Albogasio, su cui passano
ilari i vivi e i morti, salutandosi piano.

slips in and demands a hearing,
unlikely life rising off the water, still formless
yet already present, already lording
its disembodied existence over us
on our way down, and keeps climbing,
like faint smoke. Ancient steps
the steps of Albogasio, where the living and the dead
brush past one another, mumbling their hellos.

A San Mamete, con Morris. In memoria

Les dieux ont toujours soif,
n'en ont jamais assez

—GEORGES BRASSENS

È il sabato dei sabati, d'estate,
e il giorno è quasi dolce, qui sul lago.
Solo un'ondina, dunque, o il sussulto di un luccio
nell'andare svagato dei ricordi
ti riconduce tra noi, Dante, chiamandoti
dal tuo tempo scaduto. Psicopatico
paranoico, disse una volta quella bella figura
d'insegnante: quattordici? quindici anni?
Tu comunque già un bel pezzo di strada alle spalle.
Così le macerie si accumulavano,
lesioni, scricchiolii. Poi venne il gorgo
di tradimenti e pistole, il malinteso
per via dei biglietti, il morto
che forse nessuno voleva, proprio il finale
più assurdo, con la forma e il sorriso
di un cappio. Ma prima, molto prima
la ferita, nelle parole
e nei gesti: interminati
possedimenti d'ortiche. E pare in fondo
soltanto una questione di fortuna: chi l'ha avuta
e chi no. Giuseppe, Armando,
la Lucia sul balcone, a Balerna,

In San Mamete, with Morris: In Memoriam

> The gods are always thirsty,
> they can never get enough
>
> —GEORGES BRASSENS

Saturday of Saturdays, summer,
and here on the lake the day is almost gentle.
All it takes is a wavelet, then, or the leap of a pike
in the aimless shuffle of memories
to bring you back to us, Dante, to summon you
from the dregs of time. Delusional
psychopath, that paragon of teaching
called you. We were what—fourteen, fifteen?
But you'd already put a stretch of the road behind you.
Thereafter the ruins piled up—
injuries, cracks. Then came the suckhole
of backbiting and guns, a misunderstanding
over some tickets, the death
perhaps no one wanted, of all the endings
the most absurd, with the shape and smile
of a noose. But before, long before
the hurt, in word
and deed: unbroken
estates of stinging nettles. In the end it seems
no more than a matter of luck, who had it,
who didn't. Giuseppe, Armando,
Lucia on the balcony in Balerna,

quello col fucile, in cantina, e i molti altri
perduti amici, cui adesso si ripensa con stupore.
E vertigine, anche: il sentiero passava di lì.
Si respira, si annusa l'aria. Sa di glicine.

one with his rifle in the basement, the many other
friends gone and now bewildering to recall.
Dizzying, too: that way ran the trail.
Breathe, sniff the air. Smells of wisteria.

Allievi

Li incontro sulle piazze
o in qualche bar, li riconosco
quasi sempre, e penso cosa diventano,
adesso, tutti quegli occhi, quelle dita.
Carburatori, cravatte. Certi timidi,
altri perfino odiosi. E i devastati,
quelli che leccano l'asfalto.
E infine anch'io
che ho in mano cetrioli e carta igienica.

Students

I run into them in squares
or coffee shops, most of the time
I recognize them, and marvel at
what they've become:
all those eyes and fingers.
Wrenches, suits. Some shy,
others obnoxious. And the burnouts,
the ones who lick the dirt.
Then there's me,
carrying cucumbers and a roll of TP.

Signora al bar

Aveva torto a dirlo, e si perdeva,
forse, lo sguardo tra quelle nuvole basse,
malmostose, che solo molto più tardi, verso sera,
si sarebbero decise in temporale; e c'era, anche,
l'afa di giugno, i primi caldi opachi,
l'ombra di una stampella appoggiata al muro.
Ma parlava
senza rivolgersi a nessuno di preciso,
quasi con un sorriso, quasi
gentilmente, vecchia signora piena di riguardi:
"non sanno più ridere,
non come ridevamo noi, sempre col muso,
musoni come il tempo
e questo cielo."

Woman at Café

She was wrong to say so, and seemed to lose
her way, gazing up at those low, moody clouds
that would hold off until evening
before releasing rain. And there was also
the mugginess of June, the first deadening hot spells,
the shadow of a crutch propped against a wall.
But she talked
addressing no one in particular,
almost with a smile, almost
kindly, an old woman absorbed in thought.
"They've forgotten how to laugh.
They don't laugh the way we did, always moping,
mopey as the weather
and that sky."

Paesaggio

Qui piove per giorni interi, talvolta per mesi.
I sassi sono neri d'acquate,
i sentieri pesanti.

Sul bordo delle rogge:
girini, latte scure. Una valigia
incatramata.

Un filo d'olio cola
sulla ghiaia. Sopra, cemento.
Se gratti la terra: detriti,
mattoni scagliati, denti di coniglio.

Si possono pensare rumori umani,
passi, palle da tennis. Voci eventuali.
Ogni frantume è ammesso purché inutili.

Siccome questo è il vuoto c'è posto per tutto,
e quel poco che c'è, è come se non ci fosse.
Anche i binari sono perfettamente inerti,
le lucertole immobili, i vagoni
dimenticati.

E poi il pollaio. Le cose senza storia.
O fuori. Una carriola
che non ha ruote. Un pozzo. Un secchio marcio
privo di fondo. Il nome di uno scemo:

Landscape

It rains all day for days here, sometimes months.
The stones are black with rainwater,
the trails heavy-going.

Beside the canals,
tadpoles, dark cans. A suitcase
turned to tar.

A string of oil drips
over the gravel. Above, cement.
Scratch the earth and you get rubbish,
shards of brick, rabbit teeth.

Human noises come to mind,
footsteps, the pops of a tennis match.
What may be voices.
Any fragment may enter as long as it's useless.

Holes this empty leave room for everything,
and what little there is seems not there.
Even the train tracks are perfectly still,
the lizards frozen, the freight cars
forgotten.

Plus the chicken coop. Things with no history.
Or outside history. A pushcart
without wheels. A well. The rotted-through
bottom of a bucket. Luigino, a name

Luigino. Piume dentro la rete, di gallina.
Buchi dentro la rete. Trame rotte.
Quello che non chiamate crudeltà.

Io sono questo: niente.
Voglio quello che sono, fortemente.
E le parole: nessuno adesso me le ruberà.

fit for an idiot. Hen feathers in a net.
The net torn in places. Ripped mesh.
That which none of you calls cruelty.

This is what I am: nothing.
I want what I am, fiercely.
And words: now no one will rob me of them.

Bozzetti per scagliola

1

La tenda che nasconde la cucina,
i ritratti appesi, il caffè . . . *Mi manca,* dice,
*e sono io ad essermi punita. Adesso vive
qui vicino, pochi metri, ma mi manca*
(e viene dal corridoio nell'ombra una folata
come di lacrime segrete, e notti lunghe
d'insonnia) *e mi preoccupo
per lei, per la sua vita
che forse sta sciupando. E non so dire
niente, quando la vedo, e sbaglio, e dico
forse le cose sbagliate.* È ancora, e sempre,
lacerazione, questa, di parole
che non sanno parlare, di orgoglio
o d'altro schermo che ci lega, ci allontana
dal centro di noi stessi? Sopra un muro
ride la figlia andata
altrove, ride con gli occhi
o almeno così pare.

2

Melassa. A volte
sembra melassa questo tempo
che riduce ogni cosa a fanghiglia

Sketches for Scagliola

1

Curtain hiding the kitchen,
portraits hung, coffee . . . *I miss her,* she says,
*and I'm the one being punished. She lives
nearby now, just up the road, but I miss her*
(from the shadowy hall comes a whoosh of air
that sounds like muffled crying and sleepless
nights) *and I worry
for her, for the life
she seems to be squandering. Whenever I see her
I don't know what to say. I go about things wrong,
and seem to say the wrong thing.* Is that it, then,
suffering, as always, words
incapable of coming out right? Pride?
Or another condition that binds us, drives us
further from the center of ourselves? On a wall
her daughter, gone elsewhere,
is laughing with her eyes
or so it seems.

2

Schmaltz. Sometimes
it's like we're living in an age of schmaltz,
everything boiled down to private

privata. Come ogni cosa ricade
e si sfa, come ogni foglia
piange sul suo destino, e poi si smorza
e si perde in gioiosa
apatia. Ma quante storie
s'intrecciano e vana
pare ogni nostalgia d'un'altra luce.
Speranza? Forse,
se resta tempo e forza; soprattutto
la pazienza di ascoltare ogni voce.

3

Il bambino più veloce della scuola,
che non aveva mai visto una matita, figurarsi
un pastello, una gomma viola, un neocolor,
un giorno piangeva appoggiato al muretto di un bar
e un'ora dopo correva nel vento del cortile
con le sue orecchie grandi e la maglietta rosa.
Veniva da un paese travolto,
odorava di mare e di muschio e di pirite,
sicuramente era fuggito da qualcosa
e non poteva fermarsi.

4

Quei ragazzi sul piazzale
scherzosi o annoiati nel sole,
e i loro frisbee,
qualcuno li guarda dall'ombra

muck. The way everything falls
and falls apart, every leaf
laments its destiny, then abates
and gives way to the mild high
of apathy. So many stories
get tangled up, and longing
for another light appears vain.
Hope? Maybe,
if there's still time, strength, and most of all
patience to attend to each voice.

3

The fastest kid in school
who'd never seen a pencil let alone
a crayon, rubber eraser, or Neocolor wax pastel
is crying against the wall of a café one day
and an hour later he and his big ears are
sprinting through the courtyard in a pink t-shirt.
He came from a crippled country.
It smelled of the sea and moss and fool's gold.
Clearly he'd had to flee from something
and couldn't stop running.

4

That group of guys in the plaza
clowning around or bored in the sun,
them and their frisbees—
someone is almost moved as he looks on

di un'altra età quasi con commozione
e non lo sanno, ignari come stelle.

5

Angela piange perché non sa parlare,
perché non sa nessuna lingua e si sente muta,
intuisce che una catena stringe il suo silenzio
a un'esplosione di volti, il suo balbettio
a un passato che appena conosce, tormento privato
che non si può neanche raccontare
tanto è comune, e sordo. Eppure parla,
eppure sa di non saper parlare.
Per questo scoppia in lacrime, nell'ora
di biologia, davanti alla lavagna.

6

L'orecchio che ascolta non vede la voce che parla
nella notte, perduta, ma attende il brusio
dell'aria, attraverso le strade
che forse qualcuno percorre.

La voce che parla non cerca nessun ascolto,
eppure spera che il suo soliloquio non sia vano,
che un uscio l'accolga in silenzio,
offra una luce, un ramo di forsizia.

from the shadows of another age
and they have no idea, oblivious as stars.

5

Angela is crying because she can't talk,
because she has no language and feels gagged.
She senses her silence is linked to an explosion
of faces, her babble to a past she hardly knows,
a private torment so common she can't
convey it, and deaf. And yet she talks.
And yet she knows she doesn't know how to talk.
That's why, during biology,
she breaks into tears at the blackboard.

6

The ear that listens doesn't see the speaking voice
lost in the night, but waits for the rustle
of wind through the streets
someone may be walking down.

The voice that speaks expects no hearing
yet hopes its soliloquy is not in vain,
that a door will silently open
to offer light, a branch of forsythia.

Senza guardare nulla, tra rifiuti sul ciglio
e autostradali rassegnate tristezze,
vaga lo sguardo stancamente attorno, l'occhio posa
sulle scarpate e i noduli di case, rotolando,
sotto i viadotti e gli inceneritori, agli opifici
languidi nella sera. Dietro i pioppi
sfumature importune di rosso, movimenti del cielo,
strappano l'orizzonte nel momento sbagliato,
è il carro avventuroso di Fetonte
a precipizio su di noi incolonnati.

7

Looking at nothing, at refuse on the roadside
and the demoralizing sadness of highways,
the gaze wanders sleepily, the eye lingers
over escarpments and grouped houses, spinning,
under viaducts and incinerators, to the mills
idle in the evening. Behind some poplars
intrusive shades of red, movements in the sky,
tear open the horizon at the wrong moment.
It's Phaethon's adventuring chariot
looming over our column.

Il Testimone

L'avevamo convinto con difficoltà, vincendo la pigrizia e quel grumo di vergogna e paura. Non devi preoccuparti, dicevamo: bastano le cose che ci hai raccontato così spesso. Anche senza nome, anche dette male. Che almeno non sia stato inutile, non vada perduto. E gli ricordavamo i fatti che ci erano sembrati più importanti: il ghiaccio, il congelamento, la minestra di vermi a Metz, la fuga con la divisa da ufficiale, l'SS sul filobus tra Como e Cernobbio, il contrabbandiere nei boschi del confine. O certe battute, come "sparami, sparami pure", e (ma quella era venuta molto prima, c'entrava una fabbrica, una più sorda guerra) "ti sputo in faccia, ti sputo". Poi avremmo voluto sapere, in fondo, anche noi, chi aveva mosso i fili: perché, e chi si era seduto nei posti migliori, davanti all'orchestra. E che lo capisse lui, soprattutto: le vedesse, le salamandre che avevano attraversato le fiamme. Il verminaio.

All'inizio ci fu qualche problema col microfono; poi, la prova della voce. L'imbarazzo. La giornalista era gentile, capiva. Si rilassi, ripeteva, non c'è fretta; quando vuole. Ma lui, finalmente deciso, guardandola forse per la prima volta, tirando fuori la voce da un deposito abbandonato, lontanissimo, disse adagio: se ne vada. Se ne vada, per favore, subito.

Poi, credo, non se ne parlò più.

Witness

Convincing him was hard, in the end laziness and that clot of shame and fear won out. There's nothing to worry about, we said, just tell her what you've always told us. Omit the names, fumble the telling. At least it won't have been pointless, it won't be forgotten. And we reminded him of what seemed to us the most important details: the ice, the frostbite, the maggot soup in Metz, his escape in an officer's uniform, the SS on the trolley from Como to Cernobbio, the smuggler in the woods along the border. Or some of what got said, like "Shoot me, go on, shoot me" and "I spit in your face, I spit on you" (though that was much earlier, involved a factory, a secret war). For our part, we wanted to know who had pulled the strings and why and who had sat in the best seats, facing the orchestra. Most of all we wanted him to make sense of it, to see the salamanders had made it through the fire. The wormery.

At first there was a problem with the microphone; next, the sound test. Embarrassment. The journalist was kind, she understood. Relax, she kept saying, there's no rush. Whenever you're ready. And then, having finally made up his mind, looking at her for what may have been the first time, recovering his voice from a dusty, deep recess, he spoke slowly: Go away. Go away, please, this minute.

I think that was the last he spoke of it.

Palace Beach

"Como Erba, Erba Como, quante volte su e giù, sempre a piedi; che adesso, invece, con queste gambe, per via della caduta, come una scema, in cucina, spam! E non va a posto, non va; da prendere come viene, ha detto il medico, e prendiamola come viene; ma allora come un cerbiatto con quei documenti nel reggipetto. Se mi fermavano, addio. E mi hanno ben fermato, ma solo colpa di quell'invidiosa che veniva a rimpinzarsi e poi mi denunciava; perché mio padre era maresciallo e dunque la roba non mancava. Poi ero una bella ragazza, e i tedeschi qualche volta mi venivano dietro per quello; se avessero saputo! Che proprio lì dove guardavano c'erano i documenti, i volantini, i nominativi. Guardare e non toccare, gli dicevo, e ridevano. *Ja, ja.*

Una volta, qualche anno fa, ne ho visto uno, dei capi però, che mi faceva le domande in prigione: qui al mare, l'ho visto. Lei cos'ha da guardarmi, mi ha chiesto, perché mi guarda così? La guardo perché lei tanti anni fa mi ha arrestato, gli ho detto. Perché ce n'è ancora di tedeschi, vengono qui in vacanza. E di fascisti, anche. Lo sapeva?

Ma lei, cosa fa poi sempre con il libro e i fogli? Scrive le poesie?"

Palace Beach

"Como–Erba, Erba–Como. Up and down. Back and forth. Always on foot. Not anymore, not with these legs, after the stupid tumble I took in the kitchen—bam! They can't be fixed. They can't be. The doctor said to take things as they come. Well, I'm taking things as they come. But back then I was like a deer, light on my feet, with those papers tucked into my bra. If they stopped me, I was finished. And they did stop me, thanks to that jealous girl who'd come here to stuff her face and then report me. My father was the marshal, see; we didn't want for things. Plus I was pretty, so sometimes the Germans would follow me around. Had they known! They were staring right at the papers, the pamphlets, the lists of names. Look but don't touch I'd tell them, and they'd laugh. *Ja, ja.*

Once, a few years ago, I saw one of them, one of the officers who'd questioned me in prison. Here at the beach—I saw him. What are you looking at, Miss? he asked. Why are you looking at me like that? I told him: I'm looking at you because years ago you arrested me. Because there are still Germans around, they come here on vacation. Fascists too. Did you not know that?

And you—what's with all the books and papers? Are you writing poems?"

Visita Notturna

Stai sognando
cratassi, tirabraccia, il drago soffia-naso.
Chissà cosa sognava Anna Brichtova, che stanotte
viene a trovarci con il suo mosaico
di carte colorate: la sua casa
col tetto rosso, gli alberi
nel prato verde, il cielo: e fuori un lager.
Questo è il vero regalo
che ho portato da Praga senza dirtelo.
Era con me sul treno, la mattina
che ho creduto di vivere all'inferno: Stoccarda,
o giù di lì, dentro un ronzare
di gente che lavora a non so cosa
o per chi, ma lavora, preme tasti,
invia messaggi a ignoti dentro l'aria.
Solo occhi e dita, solo
un giorno dopo l'altro, smisurato
trascorrere di un tempo che non varia, che appartiene
per sempre ad altri,
ad altro che a sé stessi, e la paura, l'odio
del paria contro il paria, questa rissa
d'anime perse, nuovi schiavi. Il Grande
Bevitore di Birra, la Donna Occhi nel Vuoto,
Mazinga, i miei compagni di viaggio.
Chissà come sognava Anna Brichtova,
a cosa sogni tu, e come vedete

Night Visit

You're dreaming
of Cratoids, Armpullers, and Sneeze the Dragon.
What dreams must Anna Brichtova have dreamed?
Tonight she comes to us with her mosaic
of colored paper: her home
with its red roof, trees
in a green meadow, the sky—outside, a concentration camp.
This is the real gift
I picked up in Prague and kept secret from you.
It was with me on the train that morning
I thought I was living in hell: Stuttgart,
or south of there, inside a whirr
of people working, on what or for whom
I don't know, but working, pressing buttons,
sending messages to strangers in the air.
Nothing but eyes and fingers, nothing but
one day to the next, the yawning
passage of unvarying time, which pertains
always to others, to things
other than themselves, and fear, and hatred
of one pariah for another, this battle
of lost souls, new slaves. The Great
Beer Drinker, the Starer into Space,
Mazinger Z—my travel companions.
Who knows how Anna Brichtova dreamed,
what you dream, how you children

il mondo voi bambini. Lo troverete,
fra i vostri giochi, il gioco che ci salvi?

Noi tutti lo speriamo
guardandovi dormire.

see the world. Will you find
among your toys the toy that saves us?

We all hope so
as we watch you sleep.

Furia di Nina nei pressi di Modena

E io non sono niente di tutto questo.
Voi lo sarete: voi.
Sarete sordi, sarete muti, sarete ciechi.
Sarete una spiegazione.

Nina's Outburst, near Modena

No, I am none of those things!
You're the ones. You.
You're the deaf, the dumb, the blind.
You're the reason.

Breve omaggio a Plutone

1

Non ridiscendere. Qui
nella notte del vento,
da qualche parte nella notte, lunga
di fari e strade, Plutone
aspetta che tu sali, più in basso.
Più in basso: se resta
nel suo chiuso. Dev'essere
così: non ridiscendere, vai.
Verso i tuoi giorni, solo tuoi e di nessuno.
Verso altre notti più dolci da spezzare
come un frutto, con altri. Non ridiscendere,
vai.

2

Perché la pioggia, perché il vento e le pianure
notturne, l'erba gialla, il respiro. Quell'acqua
che scroscia nei vicoli, e i prati. Perché
non c'è tregua, o domani. Soltanto
le sbarre, la gabbia di un io.
L'inferno è non essere gli altri,
guardarli passare e sparire nel niente:
un posteggio che piano si svuota,
il cantiere del vento.

Brief Homage to Pluto

1

Don't go down again. Here,
on this windy night,
somewhere on a night of never-ending
headlights and roads, Pluto
is waiting down below for you to rise.
Down below—if he remains
in his enclosure. This is how
it must be. Don't go down again, go on.
Toward your days, yours alone and no one's.
Toward sweeter nights to divvy up
with others, like fruit. Don't go down again,
go on.

2

Because rain, because wind and valleys
at night, yellow grass, breath. That water
raking the alleys and fields. Because
there is no truce or tomorrow. Only
these bars, the cage of an I.
Hell is not being others,
watching them slip by and disappear:
a parking lot that slowly empties,
the windblown worksite.

3

Aprire la mano: questo è difficile. Lasciare
qualcosa senza sacrificio, senza
falsità. Essere il volto
che si allontana da te, l'ala che sfugge, il pianto
che non piange per te.

3

Opening your hand, that's the hard part. Releasing
something without sacrifice, without
deceit. Being the face
that fades from you, the wing that flits away, the cry
that does not cry for you.

Pietra sangue

Scaglia di gesso, polvere
impastata con l'acqua e con la colla,
il fondo nero lucente
dei colori. Anni di pietra
e silenzio, giorni persi
solo per pochi istanti luminosi. Nelle sere
d'inverno, dietro i vetri
splendono figli e animali mansueti, pane e vino
e letame da spostare, odori densi
di paglia, di fatica sprofondate nel tempo.
I boschi, i boschi! Quale voce senza voce
ne proviene, smemorata,
che radici di epoche, o sorgente
ricoperta di foglie, che sentiero
smangiato? Eccolo, il nero
di seppia della notte, il fondo cupo
che devi lucidare con pazienza, percorrendone
i pori e le vene più invisibili. Volto per volto,
amico per amico: qualcosa da custodire,
da proteggere. Concentrare la luce in pochi tratti
che svettano sul nero: il rosso, il giallo
di qualche fiore o uccello, il bianco della neve.
La forza delle pietre: sette pietre senza nome,
ma l'ultima si chiama pietra sangue.

Pietra Sangue

Plaster flake, powder
mixed with water and glue,
the black base a gloss
of pigments. Years of stone
and silence, whole days
wasted on a few brief sparks.
On winter nights, the windows
are lit with children and pets, bread and wine,
and muck to move, the strong smells
of straw, and labors sunk in time.
The woods! The woods!
What voiceless amnesiac voice issues from them?
What ancient roots? What springs
buried under leaves or eroded
path? There it is, the squid-ink
black of night, the dark base
you have to buff with patience, polishing
the faintest pores and veins. Face by face,
friend by friend: something to watch over
and protect. Gather the light in a few bands
that shine through the black: the red or yellow
of a flower or bird, white snow.
The force of stone: seven stones unnamed
but the last is called *pietra sangue*.

Folla sommersa

La memoria non si oppone affatto all'oblio. I due termini che formano contrasto sono la cancellazione (l'obblio) e la conservazione; la memoria è, sempre necessariamente, un'interazione dei due.

—TZVETAN TODOROV

Paul Hooghe, l'ultimo lanciere caduto su nessuna spiaggia,
   il superstite
delle trincee dimenticate e scomparse, su cui sorgono oggi
grandi complessi commerciali o lussuosi villaggi satellite
immersi nel verde di pitosfori, di platani le cui radici vagano
per antichi camminamenti sotterranei, il granatiere fantasma
ultracentenario spentosi a Bruxelles pochi mesi or sono,
come una piccola candela su cui passa il vento, che era stato
coscritto sedicenne di un secolo sedicenne (1916) eppure già
molto cattivo, molto crudele, ma si era ancora
al principio di tutta la storia,
alle vaghe promesse di stragi, alle belle bandiere: sapeva
di essere una curiosità, aspirava a un Guinness dei primati, a
   una targa?
E aveva memoria
lui, almeno lui, dei corpi nella notte e nel fango
straziati, mutilati, dei traccianti, sobbalzava, incompreso,
ripensando una mina saltare, una nube nervina?
Quei morti gridavano ancora grazie a lui,
dalla Marna o sul Carso?
O il nastro era già scorso, la pellicola

Buried Crowd

Remembering is not the opposite of forgetting. The two opposing terms are destruction (forgetting) and preservation. Memory can only ever be the result of their interaction.

—TZVETAN TODOROV

Paul Hooghe, the last lancer not to fall on a beach, survivor
of the forgotten and filled-in trenches, now in the shadow
of big shopping centers or lush satellite towns
ensconced in pittosporum and plane trees with roots that zigzag
through the tunnels of the past, the ghost of the grenadier
perished a few months ago in Brussels at over a hundred,
like a little candle that the wind snuffed out, conscripted
at sixteen when the century turned sixteen (1916) yet already
practiced in the arts of evil and cruelty, though that was
at the start of the story,
when the promise of slaughter was still a distant thought. Did
    he know
he was an anomaly, covet a place in the Guinness Book of World
    Records, a plaque?
A man who'd seen what he'd seen
must have remembered the bodies at night in the mud
torn apart by tracer shells, must have been blindsided
by the memory of a mine going off or a cloud of nerve gas.
Did those dead men from the Marne or on the Karst Plateau
still scream on his account?
Or had the reel already run out, the film

riavvolta e ormai illeggibile, tradotta
nel passato remoto dell'euro, o in un alzheimer? Ottant'anni
secondo gli storici perdura la memoria
viva che il mondo ha di sé: poi è deportata
in un posto dove adesso c'è Paul Hooghe, coi suoi compagni,
i ricordi che forse aveva mio padre e quelli della sua età,
tra un po' ci sarà anche mio padre e tutti i suoi amici e nemici,
una grande folla sommersa che ci guarda in silenzio e ci attende.

rolled up and illegible, translated
into the remote past of the euro, or erased by Alzheimer's?
   Eighty years,
according to historians, is how long our living
memory lasts before being deported
to the place where Paul Hooghe and his companions now
   reside,
the memories my father might have had, and those his age.
Soon my father and all his friends and enemies will join
the great buried crowd that watches in silence and waits for us.

Le prime fragole

Strisci nell'erba bianca di margherite.
Sei vestito di rosso, hai una cuffia rossa in testa,
e nella mano destra un pelacarote che infilzi
nel terreno ancora molle di marzo, sempre avanzando
lentamente nel folto del prato. Sdraiato
sull'erba, con le margherite negli occhi. Sto scalando
l'Everest, mi dici. E anche le guance sono rosse di gioia.

Strisciavi ieri nel tuo Everest di margherite
e io ti guardo oggi nel ricordo e intanto ascolto la radio
in attesa di notizie terribili, e tu continui a strisciare felice
e la radio dice della bambina schiacciata da un panzer a Gaza
tu prepari una pozione con piume d'uccello per imparare a
    volare
io ti preparo le prime fragole rosse dell'anno e mi chiedo se gli
    occhi
dell'uomo che guidava il panzer avranno capito.

First Strawberries

You're crawling in white clusters of daisies.
You're dressed in red, a red cap on your head,
and with your right hand you plunge a carrot peeler
into the mush of March, always advancing
slowly through the overgrown meadow. Lying
on the grass with daisies in your eyes. I'm climbing
Everest, you tell me. Even your cheeks are red with joy.

Yesterday you were crawling in your Everest of daisies
and today I see you in my thoughts as I listen to the radio
expecting terrible news, and you continue your happy crawl
and the radio says a child was crushed by a tank in Gaza
you prepare a potion of bird feathers that will teach you to fly
I prepare the first red strawberries of the year for you and
    wonder
if the eyes of the man driving the tank understood.

Senza immagini

Avendo da anni deciso felicemente
di rinunciare alla televisione non vedremo
la danza delle bombe su Bagdad su Bassora sui resti
di quello che un tempo fu il centro del mondo.
Non vedremo le facce gravi dei potenti
le smorfie eroiche degli inviati speciali
le scene raccapriccianti di macelli e di fuoco. No, grazie,
rinunceremo allo spettacolo. Alla festa.
Davanti alla radio, in silenzio,
potremo guardare nel vuoto, immaginare
quel che si può immaginare, troppo poco.

Senza immagini
tutto sarà più chiaro, più tremendo.

Without Images

Having happily made the decision years ago
to do without television, we will not see
the bombs dancing over Baghdad over Basra the ruins
of what was once the center of the world.
We will not see the grave faces of the powerful
the heroic winces of the special envoys
the chilling scenes of slaughter and flames. No, thanks,
we'll do without the spectacle. The party.
Sitting beside the radio, in silence,
we can stare into space and imagine
what there is to imagine, all too little.

Without images
everything will be clearer, more unbearable.

Testimonianze

Sul lavoro,
proprio niente da dire: brava gente,
scrupolosi. E mai una volta
che lei avesse fatto il bucato
se non era il suo turno.

Certo, il bambino. Scomparso nel nulla,
più o meno. Ma non è che lui
l'abbia davvero "portato via". Non so.
Lei piangeva molto, è chiaro.

Mostrava i biberon pieni di latte
nello sportello del frigo.
Perché usava la pompetta tiralatte
per via del lavoro, fino a tardi la sera.

Che la picchiasse, non si sa.
Se aveva sporto denuncia, ci sarà pure un motivo.
Ma non gridavano mai, credo.

Una volta le ho offerto un cappuccino,
siccome era scoppiata in lacrime
per strada.

Diceva così: "Che cosa ho io fatto,
che cosa ho io fatto di mia vita?
Non è uomo, quello, un animalo".

Testimonies

About work—
no complaints. They were fine people,
efficient. She never
hung her wash
out of turn.

The kid, of course. He up and vanished
more or less. But it isn't as if
the guy "abducted" him. I don't know.
She cried a lot, that's clear.

She kept her feeding bottles
in the refrigerator door.
Because she worked late
she had to pump her milk.

Did he beat her? I don't know.
She must have had her reasons for filing a complaint.
But I don't remember any scenes.

One time I bought her a coffee
after she broke down
in the street.

She would say things like, "What I do?
What I do with my life?
That one, he no man, he animal."

Due tonfi, ma poteva essere altro:
una sedia che cade, un libro.
E subito dopo un verso,
e ho pensato al cane dell'altro appartamento.
Sembrava proprio un guaíto, in effetti.

A fare più impressione è stato il telo,
quando scendevano col corpo dalle scale.
E anche i sigilli neri sulla porta.

Per ore fermi in crocchio nella strada:
una ventina, almeno, giornali, televisione.
Salivano a turno,
o telefonavano: li mandavo via. Sciacalli.

E adesso in fondo alla via, in un palazzo,
raccontano in giro che sentivano urla
da mesi. Amano il sangue
degli altri.

Poi, quando penso
a quel povero bambino.

Se ho capito bene,
aveva già avuto una storia brutta
in passato. E chissà che speranze
quando è venuta qui, in Svizzera.
A farsi ammazzare così.

Two thuds. It could have been anything:
a chair knocked over, a book dropped.
After that I heard a cry
and figured it was the dog next door.
Sounded just like dog whimpers.

The scariest part was the sheet
when they carried the body down the stairs.
That and the black tape on the door.

They camped out on the street for hours.
At least twenty of them. Papers. TV.
They took turns coming up.
Or phoned. Get lost, I'd tell them. Vultures.

Now everybody in the building down the street
goes around saying how they heard shouting
for months. They love the blood
of other people.

When I think
of that poor baby.

As far as I know
she'd been in a fix before.
Who knows what hopes
she'd pinned on Switzerland.
To get herself killed that way.

Bivio Rosales

Sale il sonno a ogni stazione, i vetri piangono.
Disporre: rivista, telefono, biglietto. *Ti ricordi?*
chiede lei allo spirito lento che si accomoda
di fronte. *Marietta, trent'anni fa, la vecchia banda*
del pub. Tu avevi i capelli lunghi lunghissimi,
io bionda. Facevo l'oroscopo, sapevo
gli ascendenti. E stavo dietro al tuo amico, uno dei pesci,
ma ho scordato il suo nome,
il suo volto. E si riprende
la corsa. I grandi fiumi
rimangono lontani: gli affluenti
gialli tagliano i prati. L'acqua striscia da selve
su brughiere imperlate,
cola tra campi di bruma e ferroviarie
trincee, stagna nei solchi.
Stingono case: il piano
è una morsa di strade e solitudini
protesa su Milano. Chiuso anche l'occhio
dei laghi, la domanda
mite degli ultimi colli di Brianza.
Condotti, direzioni di marcia
inerziali. Vivere
così, secondo ritmi
assegnati un purgatorio
di giorni. Albate, Bernate, Casnate,
Fino Mornasco, Usmate,

Rosales Junction

Sleep mounts at each station, the windows weep.
Splayed: magazine, telephone, ticket. *Remember me?*
she asks the lazy spirit taking the seat
opposite. *Marietta, thirty years ago, the old gang*
at the pub. You had the longest hair back then,
and I was blond. I did horoscopes. I knew
the rising signs. And I was following your friend, a Pisces,
but I've forgotten his name,
his face. The wheels
start to turn. The great rivers
remain back there, their yellow tributaries
bisect the meadows. Water snakes out of the woods
onto rain-dotted moors,
creeps across misty fields and railway
trenches, and stagnates in grooves.
Houses fade. The plain
is a narrow stretch of streets and lonely places
all the way to Milan. Shut, too, the eye
of the lakes and the subdued
matter of the last hills of Brianza.
Channels, inert
directions of travel. To live
according to these rhythms,
consigned to a purgatory
of days. Albate, Bernate, Casnate,
Fino Mornasco, Usmate,

Seregno, Carimate,
quasi un rosario
pendolare e in fondo
il nerofumo di Seveso, posteggi. *Valerio?*
No, l'ho perso di vista, e poi ho saputo
che è andato via, lontano, non so dove. Io ora studio
l'informatica, cosa vuoi, mi riciclo. Ma si vive.
Stride il vagone, arresta
dentro la nebbia il treno ad un semaforo. Qui un nome
vasto e severo appare, come un monito: Bivio
Rosales. Ma nessuno scende.

Seregno, Carimate—
commute as rosary—
culminating in parking lots
and the black smoke of Seveso. *Valerio?*
I lost sight of him. I heard he moved
someplace far away. I'm studying computers now.
What? I'm making a change. It's a life.
The car screeches, the train
stops at a signal in the fog. Vast, severe, a name
looms up, like a warning: Rosales
Junction. But no one gets off.

Valle dei morti

C'è una piccola valle che s'inoltra
nelle colline così dolci e popolose, solo un tratto
d'ombra visto dal treno, dietro il verde
che fugge e quelle bestie
miti, vacche e cavalli
uguali da un anno con l'altro e quasi immobili
lungo il filo dei giorni.
Ma uno, se alza gli occhi dal suo libro,
o si sveglia smarrito a uno sobbalzo,
la guarda per un attimo come si guarda il vuoto.
E tutto è fermo: una coda a mezz'aria,
un getto giallo d'urina, un ghiacciaio teso
sui fotogrammi spezzati, un bambino
che salta e resta appeso
al suo gesto giocoso. C'è una casa
e del fumo, un paesaggio tagliato dal treno.
E quell'ombra.

C'è sempre una piccola valle che s'inoltra
e non si sa dove porti
se ci passi
qualcuno mai. Lì vorrei immaginarvi
camminare da soli nei boschi d'autunno,
a modo vostro liberi, senza voltarvi. E non posso.

Valley of the Dead

There is a narrow valley that presses forward
into the rolling, densely populated hills,
no more than a band of shadow
seen from the train, beyond the greenery
going by, and the livestock,
those cows and horses,
this year the same as last, hardly budge
in the string of days.
But someone looking up from their book
or jolted awake
stares briefly into the void of that valley
and everything freezes: a tail midair,
a yellow jet of piss, a glacier poised
on torn movie stills, a child
who leaps and hangs suspended
in his playful pose. There is a house,
some smoke, a landscape bisected by the train.
And that shadow.

There is always a narrow valley that presses forward.
No one knows where it leads
or whether anyone
ever passes through. I'd like to picture you there,
walking alone in the autumn woods,
free in your way, not turning back. And I can't.

Due Aironi

1

Lago del Dosso, e nell'ambra dei prati
l'airone osserva immobile i canneti
e la nebbia, l'albergo in rovina,
l'erba folta, la stagione inoltrata e non mite,
le notizie non buone. Distante, cinereo,
se ne va a larghi giri nel grigio, con ali
vaste che battono piano nell'aria,
senza emettere voce, pacifico, lugubre, inerme.
Più temibili voli s'avvitano
ai nostri cieli autunnali,
maschere e paradossi, altre macerie
e trappole di fuoco, petrolifere
giustizie micidiali.

2

Questo fila sull'acqua come freccia scura,
che sappia dove andare e perché:
l'airone grigio, cenere dell'alba, filamento
che viene sempre dalle brume più opache dell'ovest,
dalla notte, e vola dritto verso est, dove una luce
ancora vaga si dispone, e a sé lo attrae.
Più tardi arresta il volo in una valle nascosta,
e infine calmo ripiega le ali posando sul greto

Two Herons

1

Lagh Doss, and in the amber fields
a heron stands still and studies the rushes
and mist, the hotel in disrepair,
thick clumps of grass, the season late and intemperate,
the news no good. Distant, ash-colored,
it goes in widening circles in the drear,
stroking the air with its broad wings,
producing no call, peaceful, gloomy, unguarded.
Deadlier pilots circle
our autumn skies:
masks and paradoxes, wreckage
and firetraps, killing campaigns
for oil in the name of justice.

2

This one shoots across the lake like a dark arrow
knowing where to go and what for—
gray heron, morning cinder, filament
always emerging from the thickest fog in the west,
from the night, and flying due east,
drawn that way by a dim light.
Later it lands in a hidden valley,
calmly folds its wings, and settles on a pile of stones

di un torrentello che taglia i crinali con un tuffo
tra selve desuete e rocce vive, fili a sbalzo
cadenti, copertoni e fortunosi
argini o dighe: non vere cascate,
piccoli salti, al più, brevi riposi
d'acqua in pozzetti o conche tra le pietre o vasche
da canapa o da concia abbandonate, o sgrondi
utili forse un tempo, ora insensati, rozzi scivoli;
e qui, grigio nel grigio, scende a bere,
o a poca pesca, forse, timoroso
e attento, sempre vigile, prontissimo
a risalire rapido, silente,
il corpo e le zampe allungate, le ali svelte
a cogliere il vortice d'aria delle gole,
il soffio che lo conduce più all'interno di foreste,
nel cuore di mondi perduti,
verso un'acqua che scroscia dall'alto in minuscoli rivoli
e sprofonda in terreni calcarei, marne bianche, e poi riemerge,
goccia nei prati, macchia o lieve alone
umido lungo il pallore di rocce friabili,
zampillo, occhio di lince.
E qui l'airone ti guida, qui ti lascia
stupito, a terra, e sale a picco oltre il suo zenith,
nel suo ignoto destino di bestia
timida, con le ali.

by a stream that cuts across ridges and plunges
through untrod woods, past living rock,
frayed cables, tires, and natural
dams or dykes, not actual waterfalls,
at most short spills, briefly pooling
in shallow wells or gaps between stones, in abandoned
basins for retting hemp or tanning, in drains
that may have served a purpose once
and are now useless, rudimentary chutes.
Here, a blur of gray, it descends to drink
or feed on a few fish, timid,
wary, always vigilant, braced
to take flight again, silent,
its body and feet extended, its wings
tensed to catch an updraft from the gullies,
a wind that will carry it deeper into the woods,
into the heart of lost worlds,
toward water that pours down in tiny rivulets,
breaks on limestone and marl, and reemerges
as droplets in the fields, a mark or faint ring
of moisture on pale crumbling rock,
jet of water, eye of lynx.
Here the heron leads you, here leaves you
dazed and earthbound as it soars past its zenith,
its destiny unknown:
shy beast, with wings.

Morte di un pittore

Di tanti sogni, questo ora: carlinghe
nascoste in mezzo ai campi. Ferro nero
ricoperto negli anni dal muschio,
ala spezzata.
Mai avuto niente da dire, in fondo. Niente.
Ma i colori? I colori non esistono, sappiamo,
l'occhio dipinge il mondo
di freddo o caldo, con angoscia
o speranza. Sperimentare sempre,
sperimentare speranze. Non si poteva
davvero fare di più. Con le mani e la bocca
scavare la materia,
dentro lo sterco e la rosa,
cadaverini e bambole, e quei tubi
di plastica o alluminio: un labirinto, certo,
il mio, duro e pietoso, morbido,
impietrito. Forse il grigio,
o certi azzurri in fuga; o forse ancora
la mistura dei verdi e della terra, del terreno
nudo che aspetta l'inverno. Piccole gobbe, buche:
tutto s'incrosta, adesso, si rintana
là sotto, come un tubero, resiste. Sulla neve
vedremo stecchi sparsi e brevi orme:
una bambina serena che corre e che ogni cosa

Death of a Painter

Of many dreams, now this: plane parts
buried in the fields. Black iron
blanketed with moss over the years,
a broken wing.
Never had a thing to say. Not one thing.
But colors? We know colors don't exist;
the eye will paint the world
coolly or warmly, with despair
or hope. To experiment, always.
To experiment with hope. What more
could you really do? Unearth
material with your hands and mouth,
root through shit and roses,
small corpses and dolls, those tubes
made of plastic or aluminum. My labyrinth, sure:
hard and tender, or soft
and dispassionate. Maybe gray
or certain fleeting blues. Or else
greens mixed with dirt, the bare terrain
expecting winter. Little humps, holes.
Now everything's encrusted, sheltering
underground, like a tuber; holding on. In the snow
we'll find a scattering of sticks, faint footprints:
a little girl skipping about, and whatever

tocca e ricrea danzando.
Forme nuove. Un balletto di spine.

Sguardo che si tramanda,
senza inizio né fine.

she touches she makes dance.
New forms. A ballet of thorns.

Gaze that gets passed down,
with no beginning or end.

Dopo trent'anni

Ti seguo da trent'anni mentre vaghi cercando
non sai nemmeno cosa. Sono la luce
di un'esplosione lontana, il tuo sole di ghiaccio,
due occhi spalancati sulla magrezza di un male
che apriva certe porte, o prospettive di fuga.
Diversamente: era questo l'indizio,
la rifrazione del mio raggio sulla superficie del mondo.
Voleva dire distruggere,
frugare tra gli scarti. Spossessarsi.
Voleva dire camminare con gli occhi bendati.

Ti seguo da trent'anni alta come un rapace
con il mio becco duro di nibbio, la mia vista
che sa distinguere un topolino fra le rocce
o la tua traccia barcollante sui sentieri.
Ero nei sogni che non potevi ricordare.
Ero un grido prima dell'alba, una porta chiusa,
uno zigomo che affiora sulla pelle. Il volto folle di un uomo
impiastricciato di sugo, pulsante. Ero il bagliore
di una vallata percorsa da un fiume, luccicante di fuochi.
Ero un tumore e una stella.

E non potevi guardarmi: accecavo.
Adesso, guarda. Guarda il tronco
contorto di questi ulivi che si annodano
al terreno sassoso. Guarda il mare e la costa
incisa, e il vento scuotere

Thirty Years On

For thirty years I've watched you drift about
unsure what you're searching for. I'm the light
of a distant explosion, your icy sun,
two eyes staring at a wiry pain
that opened certain doors or avenues of escape.
Differently: that was the clue,
the bend of my sunbeam on the earth's surface.
It meant *destroy*,
pick through scraps. Divest.
It meant *walk blindfold.*

For thirty years I've watched you from above
like a raptor with my hard kite's beak and eyes
that can make out a mouse in the rocks
or your tracks as you lurch along the trails.
I was in the dreams you couldn't recall.
I was a cry before sunrise, a locked door,
a bulge in the cheek. The insane face of a man
throbbing, smudged with sauce. I was the glimmer
down in a river valley, a river lit with fires.
I was a tumor and a star.

You couldn't look at me: I was blinding.
Now look. Look at the contorted trunk
of olive trees that knit
the stony ground. Look at the sea and the coastline
carved from it, and the wind rattling

ogni ramo. È la mia ala,
non medica, ti porta, ti sostiene.
Fa quasi giorno, e un'ombra, la tua ombra
striscia tra i rampicanti e le prime formiche. Solo un'ombra,
il poco che ti resta. La tua luce a rovescio.

Sono qui, per un istante posata: a rincuorarti
e a toglierti ogni speranza. Non c'è pace
nel corso delle cose e dei corpi, ma una pace
diversa brilla ovunque e ci chiama. Se vibra
sopra l'acqua o sull'erba il soffio lieve
del tempo: ecco steli dispersi, sradicati, ed ecco il turbine
leggero delle foglie che s'infiammano
e svaniscono. Guardami pure, adesso, non abbaglio.
Abbandonarsi e resistere, due fasi
identiche del sangue e del respiro, dell'inchiostro
e del foglio, come sai. Cammini, scrivi.

every branch. That's my wing.
It nurses nothing but carries and sustains you.
The day is about to begin, and a shadow, your shadow
creeps across the vines and early morning ants. Just a shadow,
the little you have left. Your light in reverse.

Here I am, settling for a second, to give you heart
and take away all hope. There is no peace
in the orbit of objects and bodies, yet everywhere
a different peace shines and calls us. There,
when the gentle breath of time ruffles the water
or grass, the stems scatter, snapped at the root.
And there, the rustle of leaves that flash
and fade away. Look at me now. I won't blind you.
You know: letting go and holding on
are the same two phases of blood and breath,
of ink and paper. Walk, write.

Poems 2010–2019

Stanze del crepuscolo

Crepuscolo. Una donna impellicciata
ne chiama un'altra sull'altro marciapiedi
come da un'altra riva, che cammina
lenta con un bambino per mano costeggiando
le luminarie di quartiere, il traffico, l'opaco
fiume di un martedì. E "No" risponde
"no grazie, ho appena fatto la merenda di Natale
all'asilo, sono piena come un uovo
di Pasqua", e si allontana ridendo
da sola alla battuta involontaria. Il bambino
la segue con aria candida e paciosa
forse sperando nei cartoni
animati o invece solo
torpidamente digerendo il pandoro.

Per strada, da un giornale abbandonato
urla la faccia del politico di turno,
dichiara: "Sono fiero
di me che rappresento
il bene del Paese. La mia è stata
comunque una grande avventura,
la nostra gente lo sa,

Twilit Stanzas

The biggest fraud places a hand on his heart,
and the dumbest brute assumes he's right.

—ANTONIO MACHADO

Twilight. A woman in furs
calls across the street as if calling
across a shore to another woman
slowly walking a boy by the hand, skirting
neighborhood lights, traffic, the murky
river of a Tuesday. "No" is her answer.
"No thanks, I just ate at the kindergarten
holiday party and I'm as stuffed as a goose—
a Christmas goose!" And she goes off
laughing at her own inadvertent joke. The boy
follows her in his innocent easygoing way,
looking forward to cartoons
or simply in a daze as he digests his cake.

On the street, from a discarded paper,
the face of this year's politician
barks: "I'm proud
of myself for representing
the good of the country.
Mine has been a hell of a run.
Our people know it,
never mind the thrashing I took

malgrado la stangata che mi sono
beccato. E gli altri,
Raus". "Sembra il Duce",
ha detto un giorno mia madre
non di lui ma di un suo simile
certo persino peggiore
o più potente e più bieco.

Dicono che in tedesco la parola Angst
copra lo spettro livido che corre
dall'ansia alla paura, con ogni sfumatura
intermedia: cieco timore, angoscia,
presentimento cupo di sventura,
cristalli rotti, roghi e il resto poi,
che consegue. Economia
semantica, riassumere
in cinque lettere tutto il venir meno
della luce. Tutto lo sprofondare
fra di noi.

at the ballot box. As for the others,
raus." "He's just like Mussolini,"
my mother said one day.
Not about him but someone like him,
someone even worse
or more powerful, more menacing.

They say in German the word *Angst*
spans the livid spectrum
from anxiety to fear, with every nuance
in between—blind terror, anguish,
an eerie sense of foreboding—
and all that follows from such feelings:
broken glass, bonfires, etc. Semantic
economy, capturing
in five letters all the lessening
of light. All that breaks down
between us.

Per un operaio precipitato

a Andy e ai suoi amici,
fra cui mia figlia

Dicembre di luce che crolla
e sprofonda in cantieri, fra scrigni e bomboniere
di perla nel cuore delle città, poi lo schianto:
era un'ombra a cadere,
null'altro che un'ombra cinese
su veli di plastica grigia,
e il suo ultimo volo un garbato disegno serale,
quasi un tratto leggero, un profilo
d'angelo in picchiata, uno schizzo inatteso
di sangue da ripulire sulle vetrine
babilonesi.

Ritto sopra un giardino sospeso nel vuoto
davanti alla notte un ragazzo
sarà l'unico a vedere. E in una mano
regge un volo di passeri e rondini, mappe del cielo;
stringe nell'altra la brevità del giorno,
i crepuscoli feroci.
Sa già cosa guardare e quando, esattamente,
e che lo sguardo fa male
se non mente.

For a Fallen Worker

To Andy and his friends,
including my daughter

December light collapsing,
plunging below construction sites in the bejeweled
and gift-wrapped hearts of cities, then the crash.
What fell was a shadow,
no more than a shadow puppet
on gray tarps,
his final flight like a pretty evening picture,
barely a brushstroke, outline
of an angel in freefall, a sudden jet
of blood to wash from the Babylonian
storefronts.

Standing in a garden that floats in the air,
facing the night, a boy
will be the only one to see. In one hand
he holds a flight of swallows and sparrows, star charts.
In his other he grips the passing day,
heartless twilights.
He knows exactly what to look for and when,
how a gaze will hurt
when it doesn't lie.

Sa che non serve a niente ma è un dovere
guardare in faccia il potere,
dire: so,
credo a quello che vedo,
vedo perché non credo,
faccio un passo di danza,
getto la mascherina,
dico no.

He knows it serves no purpose but is his duty
to look power in the face,
to say I know.
I believe what I see.
I see because I don't believe.
I do my dance.
I drop the mask.
I say no.

Trillo per Ruzika

Per far passare il tempo si parlava di Storia
e lei sorrideva bosniaca portando sul tavolo
allegrie, piccoli indizi, bottiglie e tacendo
dei suoi segreti più grandi,
forse non facili da dire e condividere. Se parla
molte lingue e nessuna, se canta
cento canzoni in una, o non canta e si muove
veloce in mezzo ai tavoli e poi scappa
in cucina, dove pare ci siano
quasi tutte le cose che contano davvero, o se ritorna,
strizza l'occhio allo storico di turno,
passa tra gli avventori e di nuovo scompare
con gli avanzi di cibo, le carcasse
di pesci e di animali e le verdure
avvizzite, scivolando
lieve fuori dal Tempo . . .

Trill for Ruzika

To pass the time we talked History
and she, a Bosnian, would smile and serve
delights, little clues, bottles, and keep
her biggest secrets to herself,
perhaps too hard to say and share. If she speaks
many tongues and none, sings
a hundred songs in one, or doesn't sing and hustles
between tables then escapes
into the kitchen, where what really matters
appears to reside, or if she returns,
winks at the latest historian on shift,
toggles between patrons, and vanishes again
with scraps, the carcasses
of fish and animals and vegetables
left to languish, slipping
gently out of Time . . .

Cani

1

Il primo cane guaiva tra le tende degli uomini
guardando nell'occhio fisso dei lupi una preistoria selvaggia
inconsapevole. Erano padre, madre,
qualcosa di perduto, foresta, nostalgia,
la lunga epoca muta alle sue spalle.
Quasi nemico, ormai, lacrima persa, libertà
rinunciata per una rischiosa alleanza.

2

Poi fuggì, tenendo basse le orecchie e la coda,
filando nello spazio insanguinato. Aveva visto
le corde stringere il cranio di Boezio, farlo esplodere,
i bastoni calare sul corpo, già senza vita forse, dilaniato.

Tutto il sapere non basta se i padroni
decidono disgrazia. Un cane lo sa bene, un uomo no.

3

Ai piedi della festa e del massacro,
sotto le tavole imbandite e le croci di dolore,
sempre guardando altrove, mesti, forse annusando
l'aria che passa tra i corpi e fugge leggera,

Dogs

1

The first would yelp around the tents of men
seeing in the stare of wolves a dull, primitive
prehistory. They were its father, its mother,
something it had lost, wild, wistfully recalled,
the long unlanguaged epoch put behind it.
Almost an enemy now, a shed tear, freedom
relinquished to form a risky pact.

2

Next it fled, ears pinned back and tail down,
spinning in bloody space. It had seen the ropes
squeeze the skull of Boethius until it cracked,
the clubs come down on his lifeless, mangled body.

No amount of knowledge will do if the masters
court disgrace. A dog knows that; a man doesn't.

3

At the foot of feasts and massacres,
under tables topped with food, under crucibles,
always looking offstage, rueful, maybe sniffing
the air that slips between bodies and fades,

minuscoli cani osservano meditabondi
movimenti che nessuno vedrà mai,
fermi sopra gli affreschi sui muri calcinate
tra gambe nude di umani affaccendati.

4

L'ultimo kantiano del Reich
era un bastardo chiamato Bobby che abbaiava
ogni mattina fra Hannover e Osnabrück
festoso quando l'appello riportava
alla luce quegli uomini pesti non più umani
ritti di fronte all'alba cinerina
e di nuovo abbaiava la sera fiutando gli spettri
tremuli che tornavano,
i gesti tormentosi degli amici,
odore di pane e fratelli. Poi scacciato
da qualche testa di morto, scomparve per sempre,
ci informa Lévinas, sui terreni ghiacciati del nord,
lasciando forse una traccia di urina sulla neve,
quasi una freccia d'oro verso l'Altro.

5

Non un re longobardo incarognito
seminatore di ingiustizia. Alboino
era un volpino screziato
uno spirito libero e gentile
sessualmente insaziabile.
Fingeva di stare in un recinto verde
proprio in fondo alla strada,

tiny dogs meditate on movements
no one will ever see, arrested in frescoes
between the bare legs of human bustle.

4

The last Kantian in the Reich
was a mutt named Bobby who would howl
every morning from Hannover to Osnabrück,
and wag his tail when roll call
summoned those broken, degraded men
into the ashy morning light
and howl in the evening at the scent of ghosts
trembling on their return,
at the cruel acts of his friends,
at the smell of bread and brothers. Later, chased off
by some death's-head, he disappeared forever,
Levinas tells us, in the icy regions of the north,
and may have left a trail of piss in the snow,
like a golden arrow pointing to the Other.

5

Not a perverse Lombard king,
a sower of injustice, Alboino
was a brindled spitz,
a kind, carefree spirit,
and sexually insatiable.
He'd pretend to keep to his yard
at the far end of the street,
but we were onto him:

ma noi lo si sapeva, recitava:
era in grado di uscire
lesto, tranquillamente.
Anche alla fine, cieco,
vagava allegro per le vie,
insidiava cagnette nei villini dei ricchi.

Il mondo era più semplice, modesto,
pareva quasi ci fosse posto per tutti.

6

Quello che rideva scuotendo le fauci
in un paesino di montagna e si strozzava.
Quello che saltellava senza una gamba
in una pineta francese, mugolando di fatica.
L'occhio umido di un altro,
la sua imbarazzante preghiera di cibo.
Il pastore Tedesco infuriate alla catena,
quel gridare frenetico, perso.
La cagna ferita
che trascinava le sue interiora nella polvere.
L'allevato nell'odio e nella guerra,
che cercava le gole.
La bava degli azzuffati, i guinzagli e le fruste.
Quello abbattuto da una fucilata,
sul fondo di un vallone.
I molti di cui non rimane memoria né nome.
Così tristemente simili a noi nella loro afflizione.

he could easily slip out
and not be caught.
Even toward the end, when he was blind,
he bounded down the streets
and badgered pooches in the villas of the rich.

The world was simpler, modest,
big enough for everybody, almost.

6

One of them in a mountain town
laughed as it shook its jowls and retched.
One of them hopped on three legs
through a French pine forest, panting.
The misty eye of another
begging embarrassingly for a bite to eat.
The furious German Shepherd on its choke-chain,
its rabid barking at the wind.
The injured bitch
dragging her entrails in the dust.
One of them, battle trained,
went for the throat.
Slobber of the brawlers. Leashes and whips.
One of them gunned down
at the bottom of a ravine.
The many of whom no memory or name is left.
How sadly they resemble us in their affliction.

Lezione di nuvole

Come ti guardano, a volte,
e che vuoto di pancia ti prende
a stare lì davanti dovendo parlare spiegare qualcosa:
come un vento che spazza e ti senti cadere
portare nell'aria sparire. Ma sei
tu, proprio tu, proprio lì,
tu che arrivi da non si sa dove, da ponti
che non esistono più, da tempeste
e che insegni le nuvole chiare
le nuvole scure
e le piogge del cuore.

*

Così il deserto, forse, la sabbia
che appena si sposta e compone
un disegno ineffabile,
se l'aria la smuove e riformula
geometrie dubitose, conche di senso precario,
ipotesi momentanee di cammino, crinali.
Nulla è sicuro, è vero. Per questo si va,
fra miraggi e speranza, con l'unica
certezza della fine e del percorso
da compiere o rinunciare. Dignità
di ogni passo barcollante, molte ombre,
segnali di tormento, infinità.

*

Cloud Lesson

The way they watch you sometimes
and the pang in your stomach you get
facing them forced to talk to explain something.
As if a wind blew through, you feel you're falling
hoisted in the air disappearing. But it's
you, just you, just there,
you who come from nowhere, from bridges
that have given way, from storms,
and teach the bright clouds
the dark clouds
and rains of the heart.

*

Likewise the desert, maybe, sand.
The moment it moves it composes
an indescribable pattern,
stirred by a breeze and re-forming
dubious shapes, hollows of unstable meaning,
momentary trails and ridges.
Nothing is fixed, true. That is why we go on,
between mirages and hope, our one
certainty the end, which path
to take or turn from. Dignity
in each faltering step, many shadows,
signs of torment, infinity.

*

Ci sono posti nei pressi delle città
dove scorrono acque sfinite
ancora quasi limpide. Hanno un colore verde,
passano in mezzo ad alberi smagriti,
a tronchi biancastri
caduti sopra le rive, a certi viottoli dove
passeggiano cani al guinzaglio, ragazzi in amore,
ciclisti, e dalle chiazze d'erba affiorano vetri
e altri resti. Le acque passano liete
anche se sanno già tutto, e vanno verso
l'inevitabile, col loro coraggio
d'acqua, elemento liquido
che deve correre al basso prima di salire.

There are places in the proximity of cities
where waters limp along,
still almost clear. A shade of green,
they flow past withered trees
and ashy trunks
fallen along the banks, a few narrow lanes
traveled by dogs on leashes, kids in love,
and bikers, where broken glass and litter
spring from the grass. The waters flow gently
despite all they know, heading toward
the inevitable, their courage
waterborne, that liquid element
which must bottom out before rising.

Nebbia

Partiti ora gli amici, la casa sembra vuota, silenziosa.

*

Fuori, è la nebbia a stringere, la nebbia di montagna che schiaccia la terra sotto una cappa bassa di freddo e umidità; le valli e le cime non si vedono, ma se ne intuisce comunque la presenza, improvvisamente quasi minacciosa, là dietro, là sopra, là in fondo, dove lo sguardo non può arrivare, nel territorio invisibile da cui giungono tuttavia folate di vento, nubi in corsa, rombi di tuono, e soprattutto acque impetuose, violente e selvagge.

La montagna è anche questo, il senso di una vita faticosa, in balìa degli elementi. Poco più in là, nella casa dei vicini, una donna è sconvolta dalla morte di suo padre, e dall'inatteso comportamento delle sorelle, che due ore dopo l'accaduto hanno cominciato a farsi a brani per via dell'eredità; è l'elemento patriarcale, mi dice quasi piangendo, che riemerge come un'eruzione di generazione in generazione. Una forma di violenza familiare, di avidità che deve aver contrassegnato il padre e gli antenati, e che ora riappare in due delle tre figlie, sconvolgendo la terza, inerme e immune, e desolata davanti al lutto e alla negazione del lutto, alla tristezza che non si può neppure vivere fino in fondo, perché lo spazio della tristezza è subito occupato dalla brama di possesso.

Senza motivo apparente, ripenso a una poesia di Sereni, Intervista a un suicida, la cui estrema negazione finale ("nulla nessuno in nessun luogo mai") mi pare qui, in questo paese un attimo prima ridente e un attimo dopo incupito dal maltempo e dai

Fog

Now that my friends have gone, the house seems empty, silent.

*

Outside, the fog closes in, a mountain fog, a cold, low-slung, damp blanket pressed against the ground; though you can't see the valleys and peaks, you can sense their presence—turned almost threatening at a moment's notice—behind it, above it, back of it, there where the eyes can't get at, in the invisible territory somehow reached by gusts of wind, passing clouds, thunderclaps, and most of all the wild, violent, savage waters.

This, too, is the meaning of a mountain: a life of hardship at the mercy of the elements. Not far from here, in my neighbors' house, a woman is in shock after the death of her father and the unexpected behavior of her sisters, who, two hours after he'd died, had begun to squabble over their inheritance. It's the patriarchal strain, she says on the verge of crying, that erupts from generation to generation. A form of family violence and greed, which must have characterized her father and ancestors, and has now resurfaced in two of the three sisters and shocked the third, who is helpless and immune, rattled by her grief and the grief denied her, by the sadness she can't fully inhabit because the room for her sadness was immediately filled by their itch for ownership.

For no apparent reason, I think of a poem by Vittorio Sereni, "Interview with a Suicide," and its final extreme string of no's ("nothing no one in no place never"), which here, in this country— lovely one moment and the next clouded by bad weather and dark

brutti pensieri, ancora più comprensibile, ancora più atroce e vera.

*

Gli animali del maltempo: la cornacchia, il corvo, le lumache, le cento mosche intontite. La salamandra nera immobile sulla pietra bagnata fuori casa, e il suo piccolo occhio di vertigine, acquoso.

*

E adesso una capra bela, nel prato qui accanto. È una piccola capra di montagna, pezzata, agile, e svelta. Ce ne sono dodici nel recinto, ma una soltanto è priva di corna; sono state recise, forse per impedirle di ferire le compagne, forse perché era troppo nervosa o esuberante. Era del resto proprio lei, pochi giorni fa, a vagare libera e come stupita fuori dal recinto, che aveva forse scavalcato con un balzo, e nel quale, non senza fatica, l'ho rimessa, sollevandola. Mentre la tenevo sulle braccia, scalciava contro il mio stomaco, senza riuscire a farmi davvero male. Mi guarda, adesso, quando mi avvicino al piccolo branco? E se realmente mi riconosce: cosa pensa, se pensa, del mio gesto che voleva essere pietoso?

*

Sto facendo, si capisce, quello che di solito mi vieto di fare: scrivere liberamente, senza un filo logico, lasciando che le parole si chiamino da sole, quasi liberamente e quasi al di fuori del mio controllo.

Gioco pericoloso, forse vano, che proprio la nebbia invita a fare, occultando le cose. Modo di richiamare ciò che è assente, o più probabilmente di illudersi.

thoughts—seems to me even more comprehensible, even more atrocious and true.

*

The bad-weather animals: the rook, the crow, the snails, the hundred groggy flies. The black salamander limp on the wet stone outside my house; its small, vertiginous, watery eye.

*

Now a nanny goat, bleating in a nearby field. A small mountain goat, spotted, agile, and quick. There are twelve of them in the pen but only one has no horns; maybe they were cut to keep her from injuring the others, or because she was jumpy or excitable. A few days ago I found her wandering in a daze outside the pen—she must have cleared the fence—and struggled to lift her up and put her back inside. As I held her in my arms, she kicked at my stomach, but failed to hurt me much. Is she eyeing me now as I approach her small herd? And if she really does recognize me, what does she think, if she thinks anything, of my action which was meant to be compassionate?

*

I'm doing, you see, what I usually prohibit myself from doing: writing freely, following no logic, letting the words emerge on their own, almost free, almost beyond my control.

Dangerous game, vain maybe, which the fog itself, occluding things, invites me to play. A way of summoning what is absent, or, more likely, of deceiving oneself.

*

Le due aquile sopra il prato delle marmotte, pochi giorni fa, il loro volteggio minaccioso, inquietante. Il "terribile mondo degli uccelli" di cui parlava un verso di Omero; ma in un'altra occasione, la cincia (se davvero era una cincia) con l'ala spezzata, che fuggiva saltellando nei pascoli, tra i ciuffi di erbe grasse, terrorizzata. Impossibile aiutarla. E forse la pietà più grande sarebbe stato ucciderla subito. Ma come fare?

*

E basta uno squarcio tra le nuvole a cambiare tutto, un po' di luce a colorare il mondo. Ma basta, poi?

*

Two eagles above a field of marmots, a few days ago, their disqui-
eting, ominous circling. The "terrible world of birds," as a line of
Homer has it. On another occasion, a titmouse (if that is what it
was) with a broken wing was hopping away across the pastures,
over clumps of succulents, terrified. There was nothing I could do
to help it. Maybe the most compassionate thing would have been
to kill it immediately. But how?

*

All it takes is a break in the clouds to change everything, a little
light to color the world. That's all, is it?

Sabbia

Tu non lo sai, ma io spesso mi sveglio di notte,
rimango a lungo sdraiato nel buio
e ti ascolto dormire lì accanto, come un cane
sulla riva di un'acqua lenta da cui salgono
ombre e riflessi, farfalle silenziose.
Stanotte parlavi nel sonno,
con dei lamenti quasi, dicendo di un muro
troppo alto per scendere sotto, verso il mare
che tu sola vedevi, lontano splendente.
Per gioco ti ho mormorato di stare tranquilla,
non era poi così alto, potevamo anche farcela.
Tu hai chiesto
se in basso ci fosse sabbia ad aspettarci,
o roccia nera.
Sabbia, ho risposto, sabbia. E nel tuo sogno
forse ci siamo tuffati.

Sand

You don't know this, but often I wake at night.
I lie next to you a long time in the dark
and listen to you sleep, like a dog
on the banks of slow-moving waters that cast
shadows and reflections, noiseless butterflies.
Tonight you were talking in your sleep,
almost moaning as you spoke about a wall
too high to climb down, near a sea
only you saw, a glint in the offing.
Joking, I whispered, "Don't worry, it's
not that high, we might just make it."
You asked if
below we could expect to find sand
or black rock.
Sand, I answered, sand. And in your dream
maybe we dove.

Presenze

Informe sulla pietra litografica vaghissimo
il fantasma rimane di qualcosa, l'invisibile
sospetto esausto di senso,
splendido un tempo e perso ora, la traccia
immateriale che inquieta le stampe e le sommuove,
come un'ombra o un ricordo di luce quando invade
le nostre opere e i giorni e dice altro,
altra luce più grande
con voce incomprensibile. Così può capitare
di scorgere presenze sopra scale,
figure inesistenti lungo moli deserti o affollati,
inafferrabili volti ai finestrini di un tram.

Allora il giorno è cavo, il cielo stretto,
privo di gioia il mondo per un poco.

Presences

Formless, faint, the ghost of something
is left on the lithography stone, an invisible
spent suggestion of meaning—
once splendid, now lost—an immaterial
trace that haunts the prints and troubles them,
like a shadow or recollection of light when it invades
our works and days and speaks of something else,
a different, larger light,
in a voice we can't comprehend. The way, on occasion,
we glimpse presences on the stairs,
imaginary figures on abandoned or crowded wharfs,
faces streaking by in the windows of a tram.

Then the day empties, clouds huddle,
the world is joyless for a while.

Corpo stellare

Mi segui con un pensiero, sei un pensiero
che non devo nemmeno pensare, come un brivido
mi strini piano la pelle, muove gli occhi
verso un punto chiaro di luce. Sei un ricordo
perduto e luminoso, sei il mio sogno
senza sogno e senza ricordi, la porta che chiude
e apre sulla corrente di un fiume impetuoso. Sei una cosa
che nessuna parola può dire e che in ogni parola
risuona come l'eco di un lento respiro, sei il mio vento
di foglie e primavere, la voce che chiama
da un posto che non so e riconosco e che è mio.
Sei l'ululato di un lupo, la voce del cervo
vivo e ferito a morte. Il mio corpo stellare.

Stellar Body

You pursue me with a thought, are a thought
that comes to me without thinking, like a shiver
you slowly scorch my skin and lead my eyes
toward a clear point of light. You're a memory
retrieved and glowing, you're my dream
beyond dreams and memories, the door that closes
and opens onto a wild river. You're something
no word can express, and in every word you resonate
like the echo of a slow exhale, you're my wind
rustling the spring foliage, the voice that calls
from a place I do not know but recognize as mine.
You're the howl of a wolf, the voice of the deer
alive and mortally wounded. My stellar body.

Il Respiro di Ermanno

Caro Ermanno, ho ascoltato
un poeta polacco di nome Jaroslaw Mikolajewski
leggere una poesia che parlava del fiato,
del respiro del padre scomparso trovato in cantina
con stupore, dentro un materassino gonfiabile
di trent'anni prima.

Il fiato, pensa, la cosa più fragile, resta
di un uomo talvolta, nei luoghi più strani, e nel fiato
galleggiano forse miriadi di quei moscerini
che ti parevano lieti, o altre forme disperse

come piccoli punti di voce.

Anche tu ci hai lasciato un respiro,
Ermanno, un respiro e dei versi.

Ermanno's Breath

Dear Ermanno, I heard
a Polish poet named Jarosław Mikołajewski
read a poem that spoke of breath,
about the shock of finding his dead father's breath
in an inflatable mattress in the basement
from thirty years before.

Breath, think about it, sometimes the wispiest part of
a man lingers in the strangest places, and in that breath
maybe there floats a multitude of those gnats
you thought looked glad, or other dispersed shapes

like pinpricks of a voice.

You too left us a breath,
Ermanno, a breath and some verse.

Fantasmi a un concerto di Terry Blue

Fosse stato lì accanto nella notte,
davvero lì non solo proiezione
o fantasma, la mano già pronta
al pacchetto, all'accendino, come un tempo,
ma con l'aria di chi adesso arriva da molto lontano,
smagrito forse dagli eoni
traversati; fosse stato
lì davvero nelle tenebre corse dai fari
—la massicciata cupa le distanti
rotaie quei vecchi solchi
fangosi d'abbandono
reti spinate garitte in disuso—
suona bene però, avrebbe detto,
e sembra forte, contento di essere qui,
esattamente al suo posto, mi pare:

(del nipote questo avrebbe detto,
del figlio di suo figlio cioè mio, per lui di là
ancora da venire, inconosciuto
neppure immaginabile alla morte
prematura, del nipote sul palco ora, nel cuore
dell'antico disastro per fortuna non suo,
o di un nuovo disastro anche più duro
solo suo e non più nostro, *sweet pain*
d'alberi in fiamme e piogge, diciottenne
e nuovo secolo millennio paesaggio dolore futuro,
con me già più simile all'altro, forse, lo scomparso

Ghosts at a Terry Blue Concert

Had he been there with me that night,
had it really been him and not a projection
or ghost, his hand already reaching
for his pack and lighter, as in the past,
except now he seemed to have come from a great distance
and grown thin after traveling for ages.
Had he been there for real in the dark
crisscrossed with stage lights
—gloomy ballast train tracks
in the offing those old forgotten
muddy furrows
barbed wire abandoned sentry boxes—
he would have said, "The kid can play,
and looks tough, happy to be here,
right where he should be, I think."

He'd have been talking about his grandson,
the son of his son, *my* son, who for him
had yet to be born, whom he'd never known,
never even imagined at the time of his death,
about his grandson now on stage, in the heart
of the old disaster that he was lucky to have
no hand in, or of a new and harder disaster,
his alone and not ours, "sweet pain"
of burning trees and floods, eighteen
in a new century millennium landscape grief future.
To me, who may have more in common

mio padre, più vicino almeno per età,
con me che senza esitare forse avrei accettato
la sigaretta, il miracolo, la voce
arrochita) e avrei risposto
sì, suona bene e almeno un po'
ci riscatta. Magari ne valeva la pena, cosa dici?

Cosa dire non so, avrebbe detto sardonico,
ma vieni qua, che accendo, e poi fumiamo,
Scemenza. Dopo sarebbe andato verso il buio,
sparendo oltre quell'acqua che nel nome
ricorda i bachi morti, verso i boschi
neri di lontananza. E anch'io sarei
tornato, nella musica
pulsante dolceamara del presente. Senza
troppa paura, senza pena.

with my dead father. Am closer at least in age.
To me, who wouldn't have hesitated to accept
the cigarette, the miracle, the gruff voice.
And I'd have answered, "It's true,
he plays well, and at least he makes
some money. Maybe it was worth it. What do you think?"

"I don't know what to think," he'd have said sardonically.
"Come here, I'll give you a light, let's smoke,
Jackass." Afterward he'd have drifted into the dark,
disappeared beyond that water whose name
calls to mind dead silkworms, into the black
woods in the distance. And I, too, would have
turned back to the pulsing
bittersweet music of the present. Mostly
unafraid and untroubled.

Storia della lingua

A Patrizia

A Chiasso, in un cortile
qualunque dentro gli ultimi
anni '50 bimbi
giocano arrampicandosi
sui tralicci per battere i tappeti
nel fiato d'erba e ferro.
Eterno il pomeriggio, inarrestabili
i cirri lungo il cielo a pecorelle,
inarrestabili i giochi.
Salgono su si appendono
a gancio coi ginocchi sulle sbarre
la testa in giù le braccia a penzoloni
e con le loro garrule
vocine urlano al mondo
siamo scimmie
belle bertucce brune oranghi tanghi,
siamo scimmiette che fanno la petàce
e ridono nel tardo dopoguerra.
"Petacci" li corregge
altissima una mamma non immemore.
"Giocate pure allegri non fatevi male,
però si dice fare la Petacci: e ricordatevi
che lei non era sola
a dondolare".

History of Language

To Patrizia

In Chiasso, in an anonymous
courtyard at the close
of the '50s, kids
play, scaling
fences and beating rugs
in a puff of iron and grass.
The afternoon undying. Relentless
sheep-shaped clouds in the sky.
Relentless games.
They climb the fence and hook
their knees over the crossbeams
heads down arms dangling
and in their irrepressible
small voices shout
we're monkeys
beautiful brown apes orango-tangos
tiny monkeys doing the *Petash*
and laugh in the late postwar period.
"Petacci!" they're corrected
by a mother with a long memory.
"Play all you want, don't hurt yourselves,
but it's called 'Do the Petacci.' And remember,
she wasn't the only one
to hang."

Giardiniere

Chino sull'erba, raccogli invecchiato le foglie autunnali
con un rastrello piccolo e un giubbotto
che grida il suo arancione. Canticchi qualcosa.
Per questo non puoi vedere la mia mano
che ti salute dall'auto. Né, forse,
ricorderai l'antica ragione che muove al saluto
più che fraterno. Eravamo in un prato,
d'estate, e indosso avevamo divise
non ancora ufficiali: tute blu, da lavoro,
mestissime. Tu, quando l'istruttore
fece esplodere il secchio e ridendo sguaiato
disse che questo fa un ventre se è pieno di birra
a colpirlo come si deve, che scoppia e si muore,
tu non applaudivi vociando come la ciurma degli altri.
Piangevi dirotto. E io, nel mio inverno inchiodato,
ti abbracciavo.

Gardener

Crouched in the yard, mellowed, you gather autumn leaves
with a tiny rake, wearing a loud orange jacket.
You're humming something.
That's why you can't see my hand
waving from the car. Nor, maybe,
remember the old reason that prompts the extra
brotherly way I wave. We were in a field
one summer wearing uniforms
not yet official. The saddest blue
workers' coveralls. When the instructor
blasted the bucket and let out a vulgar laugh,
saying that was what a bellyful of beer did
if struck right, burst and died,
you didn't join the rest of the crew in a howl of applause.
You wept. And I, in my nailed-down winter,
held you.

Da un lontano Natale

Dice che appena un'ombra a lei rimane
del padre ridotto a zero dalla tisi
presto divelto non solo dall'elenco dei vivi
ma dai nomi della memoria,
come una storia abrasa perduta mai esistita:
un giardino azzurro di gelo, un paese
rappreso su colli boschivi alti su un lago,
e, calda, nel giardino
nel paese sulle colline in mezzo al mondo
nel cosmo nel secolo breve
la mano festosa di lui che compatta la neve,
dà forma umana al pupazzo
affonda una carota come naso
due monete per gli occhi
poi rientra e scompare
per sempre nel suo cielo d'incertezza.

Doveva essere il Natale
del '30 o del '31.
Nessuno, oltre mia madre, può vedere
nel fondo vago degli occhi quella mano.

Christmas Past

She says that all that's left is a shadow
of her father, ground to nothing by TB,
soon to be removed from the list of the living
and the names of the remembered,
like a story erased from existence:
a yard of blue ice, a village
huddled in the woodland hills above a lake,
and, warm, in the yard
in the village in the hills in the middle of the world
in the cosmos in the short century
his merry hand is packing snow,
turning snow into a man,
placing a carrot for the nose
a pair of coins for eyes
before he goes back in and disappears
forever in his heaven of uncertainty.

It must have been Christmas,
'30 or '31.
No one besides my mother can see
in the blurry back of her eyes that hand.

Salendo al Cristallina

Aveva ragione il padre dell'amico,
tuba o flicorno nella banda del paese,
cercatore di radici e castagne,
che conducendoci in alto, verso un posto fuorivia
dal nome cosí chiaro, Capanna Cristallina,
che solo a pensarci pareva
d'essere più leggeri nell'intrico
di rocce e bassi tronchi dell'ascesa,
ci diceva ansimando di ascoltare
i veri Quadri di un'esposizione, e non badare
alle copie moderne scalcagnate.
Certo che aveva ragione, e un gran bel passo.
Ma la voce di Greg Lake e quel pizzicato
di chitarra lancinante, quel rombo lontano,
moog batteria catastrofe cascata,
l'ombra cupa del basso,
la pianola impazzita accoltellata,
il rullato di Palmer ...

Lui del resto le radici in cantina
le copriva di copale luccicante.
Noi invece eravamo ragazzi,
affamati di tutto.

Climbing to Cristallina

He had a point, our friend's father,
tuba or flugelhorn in the town band,
forager of tree roots and chestnuts,
guiding us up to an out-of-the-way
lodge called Cristallina, a name so clear
the mere thought of it made you feel
lighter in the tangle
of rocks and stunted trees along the climb,
when he told us, panting, to listen
to the real Pictures at an Exhibition and scrap
those second-rate modern imitators.
He had a point, and moved at an awesome clip.
Still, Greg Lake's voice and that lacerating
guitar pizzicato, that distant throbbing,
catastrophic cascading Moog drummer,
moody shadow of the bass,
manic stabbing of the keyboard,
Palmer's drum lick . . .

Back in his basement,
he'd shine his roots with copal resin.
But we were kids,
starved for everything.

Dialogo di marzo

"Non puoi chiedermi di essere
come te" disse lei con un accenno
di stizza volendo
dire una limpida cosa,
quel modo di affrontare
l'eventuale contrasto o anche l'ansia
di fare ordine opporsi non cedere
così diverso dal suo,
di modo. Ma
lui si sentiva già stretto
in un'altra camicia di forza. "Neppure
io come me stesso, né voglio
o mai ho voluto. Una cenere
negli occhi, e sempre il dubbio
di non essere davvero presente, all'altezza.
E poi il dovere".

Fuori passavano le solite
essenze quotidiane, molte forme
di vita definita forse definitiva,
i ciliegi giapponesi raggiavano sterili,
nell'incoscienza di sé,
tutto quell'ingannevole rosa.

March Dialogue

"You can't ask me to be
like you," she said, slightly miffed,
by which she meant
something clear, limpid,
his way of heading off
arguments or his urge
to create order, take a stand, give no ground,
so unlike her
and her ways. But
he was already chafing
inside another straitjacket. "I'm not
like me either. I don't want that
and never have. The smoke
in my eyes, the nagging doubt
I'm not really present or measuring up.
And the feeling that I have to."

Outside the usual ordinary essences
were streaming by: many forms
of well-defined, perhaps definitive life.
The fruitless Japanese blossoms blazed up
unselfconsciously,
all that deceitful pink.

Intorno a un'antica domanda

"No" devi aver risposto. Ma
la bimba o ragazzina
dal folto di una sala
gremita e ora dal molo
lungo della memoria che chiedeva
alta come chiarissima
betulla in una landa sconfinata
"e in cosa credi, allora?",
e stava ferma poi
in piedi ad aspettare una risposta,
immobile nel vento
delle parole e del senso:
che cosa le hai potuto
rispondere?

Soltanto che un sentiero
sopra un villaggio qualunque, già ingombrato
dai rovi, che saliva
verso un altro anche più piccolo
villaggio, acciottolato
in epoche remote e ora percorso
da pochi o pochissimi,
offriva a certe curve
a certe soste del salire
i resti di antiche cappelle votive o stazioni,
una via crucis cancellata dal tempo
senza immagini e ormai quasi

Concerning an Old Question

"No" must have been your answer. But
the child or girl
emerging from a crowded room
and now from the long pier of memory
tall and bright
as a birch tree in an open field
was asking
"What do you believe in then?"
and she stood still
waiting for an answer
unmoved in the wind
of words and meaning—
how else could you
have answered?

Except to say that a path
behind a small town, buried
in bramble, which led
up to an even smaller
town, paved
in the distant past and now traveled
by next to no one,
revealed at certain bends
and stops along the climb
vestiges of an old chapel or prayer station,
a way of the cross erased by time.
No images, by now

rovina. Solo
lo spazio intonacato di un disegno scomparso
o ancora da immaginare: spazio vuoto
ma chiuso in una nicchia,
traccia di sacro laico,
segreto che non salva e non promette
eppure chiede qualcosa. Custodirlo
e non cedere, difenderlo
senza decorazioni o simulacri: puro spazio
da lasciare così, come voragine vuota
da guardare in silenzio. Questo, forse.
E, lì davanti: tutti.
Sporti sopra quel vuoto di vertigine,
con le comuni fatiche e miserie, con i sogni
e i dolori. Tutti uguali di fronte
al grigiore del nulla. Attraversati
da un'assenza che interroga e apre
domande come ferite e che fa splendere
il poco che ci è dato, la bellezza
di essere, nel tempo. Il lancinante.

almost a ruin. Just
space that had once been or had yet to be
painted, empty space
enclosed in a niche,
remnant of a secular shrine,
a secret that won't save us
but asks that we guard it,
that we go on, that we defend it
not with decorations or idols
but by keeping it pure space,
a void to stare at in silence. That, maybe.
And up ahead: everyone.
You lean out over that vertiginous space
feeling the same struggles and deprivations,
dreams and griefs. All equal in the face of
that gray nothingness. Thread
with an absence that questions and pries
open wounds and pours a light onto
what little we are given, the beauty
of being, in time. What pain.

Fiore, dirupo

Sarà stato un mattino, uno solo: qualcosa
come una luce inattesa irradiante
dietro o sotto le nuvole, una rosa disteso
lì fermo davanti al tuo giorno, magari difficile, cupo.

L'audacia dello sguardo: questo ti fu rivelato.

E dopo: essere fedele o tradire
quell'ipotesi di luce. Tutto
sommato non molto di più.
Fa' i tuoi conti, respira o distogli
lo sguardo da ciò che ferisce, richiama e ti scruta.

Il tuo mucchietto di lucciole, il tuo mucchietto di cenere.

Pesali. Fiore e dirupo.

Flower, Cliff

It must have been a morning, just one: something
like an unexpected, radiant light
behind or below the clouds, a stretch of pink
fixed before your (maybe hard, somber) day ahead.

The audacity of looking. That's what was revealed to you.

And after: to be true to or betray
that potential light.
Little more than that.
Reckon up, breathe, or look
away from what hurts, summons and scrutinizes you.

Your pinch of fireflies, your pinch of ashes.

Weigh them. Flower and cliff.

Luce invernale

Poi finalmente si è fatto vivo il vento
da giorni e giorni in agguato dietro ai boschi:
era, prima di giungere, una luce
dura scartavetrata dentro l'aria
immobile. Ogni cosa pungeva, e da ogni margine
salivano immagini estreme, alberi visti
come da un ultimo sguardo, tagli obliqui
di polvere accecante, solitudini.

Tutto sembrava un addio: costoni alti
scissi in triangoli gialli, lame d'acqua
metalliche e lanuggini
inerti, forse di nebbie in dissolvenza,
forse di fumi lontani.
Gli occhi si socchiudevano irritati,
per colmo di bellezza o d'ozono diffuso
ovunque in quel bagliore d'inquietudine.

Ma il vento ha portato l'incendio che covava
attizzando braci invisibili, fuochi nascosti
tra i faggi, ha detto la verità, accavallato le onde
e alzato in volo gli stormi di folaghe.
Il soffio d'arsura è sceso dalle coste,
a volo per le strettoie si è gonfiato sul lago
entrando attraverso fessure, spifferi, pori
fino all'intrico dei nervi e fino ai cuori.

Winter Light

At last the wind turned up
having lurked behind the woods for days.
Before it reached us it was a light
like sandpaper in the still air.
Everything stung, and strange images
emerged from every corner, trees seen
as if for the last time, oblique angles
of blinding dust, lonely landscapes.

It all seemed to say goodbye: tall crags
divided into yellow triangles, blades
of metallic water and a lingering fluff
or down that may have been the mist
lifting or distant smoke.
Your irritated eyes had to squint
at so much beauty, or from the ozone
sprawled in that unnerving glare.

But the wind brought smoldering fires,
fanned unseen embers and flames
hidden in the beech trees, told the truth,
rode the waves and sent rafts of coots flying.
A hot breeze came from the coasts,
winged down alleys, blew over the lake,
and slipped through cracks, drafts, pores,
into the knot of nerves and on into the heart.

Si è preso tutto, il vento, dolori e nostalgia,
sogni e speranze, quiete. Ci ha lasciato
bottiglie sopra i prati, sparsi giorni
increduli, stremati. È andato via.

The wind took everything away: pain and longing,
hopes and dreams. Calm. It left behind
bottles strewn about the fields, a string of days
in disbelief, shattered. And it was gone.

Stelle di calcite

Scivola verso il basso della pagina
come spossata la mano del maestro

si addentra nel margine nel biancore del vuoto
entra nell'ombra la parola dell'amico

non regge più la penna
lettere scoscese corde penzolanti frane

tra poco forse muoverà dei passi
nel corridoio del deserto

nella faglia, dove la linea di frattura
scende alle grotte nere

senza voltarsi indietro
ma gettando una luce alle spalle

come di candela tremante
invita a resistere a camminare

a cercare la strada giusta mantenendosi
in vista dell'alto se possibile

illuminati d'armonia
desiderosi di salire lungo il vento

abbassandosi al di sotto della terra se è necessario
per incontrare le concrezioni eccentriche

Calcite Stars

As if diminished the master's hand
unravels down the page

encroaches on the margins and white space
my friend's word retreats into the shadows

he can't hold up his pen
jagged letters dangling ropes mudslides

maybe soon he'll shuffle forward
down the desert corridor

into the fault where the fracture line
descends to black caves

and not look back
but cast a light behind him

that quivers like candlelight
he invites us to press on to walk

to seek the right path to remain
in view from above if we can

harmoniously lit
eager to climb along the wind

and lower ourselves into the earth if need be
to see the strange rock formations

le stelle bianche perse che sfavillano
i cristalli di calcite

dentro il buio.

the buried white stars that shine
calcite crystals

in the dark.

Libellula

1

Come perdutamente taciturno
l'occhio verde così verde del piccolo lago,
d'un verde tanto improbabile, chiaro
di sabbie e folti canneti (e l'acqua
nel fermo immagine tace, si raggela
in superficie attonita o stranita,
chissà), dove si annullano grida
e rumori distanti di traffico,
arrochiti. Bene bene,
qui è tutto perfetto, finalmente, tutto
precisamente riassumibile e in pace:
le case sopra i colli, i luminosi deserti villaggi,
gli orti e i giardini elettricamente isolati,
ogni cosa ha il suo avverbio preciso che delimita
la portata dell'azione, il delicato
definitivo ringhio del silenzio. Quelli
che qui camminano sanno
da sempre qual è la giusta direzione: cavalli,
biciclette, tutine da jogging,
yuk yuk, mumble mumble. L'armonia
è questa, dunque? L'equilibrio è nel vuoto
del senso, nella saggia
rinuncia all'incertezza dei venti
che scompigliano le praterie?
O pensi sia una questione d'età,

Dragonfly

1

How hopelessly cut off from words,
the green eye of the little lake, so green
its green appears improbable, brightened
by sandbars and thick reeds (the frozen
image of water falling silent, its surface
struck dumb or, who knows,
in a daze), where cries are buffered
and the distant noise of traffic
faint. Good, good,
at last this place is perfect, all of it
accurately drawn and at peace:
houses in the hills, empty lit towns,
gardens and lawns electrically fenced—
to each thing a specific adverb defining
what action it performs, the delicate
definitive brooding silence. Those
who walk this place have
always known which way to go: horses,
bicycles, running shorts,
ah-hyuck, hoo hoo hoo hoo. Harmony—
is this it? Is equilibrium found
in the absence of meaning, in the wise
surrender to the uncertain winds
that pick apart the plains?
Or do you think it's a question of age,

l'epoca della storia o della vita? Questo pensi?
Tappe del progresso, esitazioni del mondo,
rappezzi e rammendi del cielo?
Questo pensano gli ameni viandanti che sorridono
e si scansano appena se intercettano
il dubbio di un'occhiata che sta in bilico
sopra un gorghetto che è meglio non guardare?
E tu, cosa vuoi, per finire? Con il tuo sonno
arretrato, la stanchezza del sangue, e quel modo
di non desiderare più nulla
o quasi nulla? Cosa sai ancora chiedere
ai giorni, e in che gironi
di quale purgatorio ti incammini
controvoglia, a testa china e questa volta
a passi lenti e in fondo in fondo rassegnato
a non scoprire altre terre se non questa
labirintite prealpina? Poi:
dica con precisione il soggetto
da quanti anni decenni ore minuti secondi
vaga senza meta precisa e senza
sapere perché; dica se crede
onestamente che sia la cosa logica
o anche solo lontanamente scusabile. Dica
chi si crede dove pensa di andare
fin dove e se davvero
non riconosce in sé coscienza d'errore,
inanità di sforzi a ben vedere ridicoli.
Ponga il capo alla fine
mitemente sul ceppo e nessuna
lama cadrà, stia certo. Riconosca, riconosca,
sorrida.

historical moment or moment in one's life?
Is that what you think?
Stages of progress, waverings of the world,
stitches and patches of the sky?
Is that what the cheerful drifters think as they smile
and barely sidestep the dubious sight
they've stumbled onto, hanging in the balance
above a whirlpool—better not to look?
And what is it you want in the end?
Short on sleep, the ache in your blood, that way
you have of desiring nothing anymore
or almost nothing. What more can you ask
of the days, and in what circles
of which purgatory do you walk
against your will, head bowed, and this time
shuffling your feet, and at bottom resigned
to discover no other lands but this
labyrinth at the edge of the Alps? Then:
Will the defendant state for the record
how many years decades hours minutes seconds
he has wandered with no real purpose, not
knowing why? If he honestly believes
that is the logical thing to do
or is remotely excusable, let him say so. Say
who he thinks he is where he thinks he's going
how far and if indeed he doesn't
recognize the error of his ways,
his inane—on closer inspection absurd—efforts.
Let him lay his head
gently on the stump. Rest easy,
no blade will fall. Admit it, admit it,
smile.

2

Uno che qui abitasse, ogni mattino alzandosi,
dovrebbe dunque bearsi della luce
serena, nuvolette specchiati, cerbiatti,
inoffensive dolcezze. Regole chiare:
che le cose siano tutte orizzontali,
le curvature morbide e limitate nel tempo,
le buche e le caverne riempite di ghiaia e sigillate,
i materiali assolutamente prevedibili,
i movimenti esatti, definiti, anche dei cuori.
E allora riconosco, riconosco,
segretamente scavo, frugo nel terriccio
dei nostri anni di plastica, in un reticolo
di arterie e vene. No, nessuna via di fuga,
su questo almeno possiamo andare d'accordo. Nessuna.
Una volta c'era quel tale
che affilava coltelli su una mola,
alle pendici dei boschi: il disco grigio, abbagliante
che girava, e la lama sottile
a prendere e riflettere la luce dell'ultimo sole,
e poteva sembrare una promessa;
poi l'altro, barcaiolo o passatore
d'anime, che leggeva le piste sulle foglie
d'ottobre o di novembre, poi il profeta
silenzioso, quelle voci
negate o rinnegate, di speranza . . . Tutti andati,
inghiotti o fatti pietra.
E adesso, in questo estremo ultimo autunno,
eccola qui improvvisa,
senza bagliore o ronzio per annunciarla,

2

One who lives here, rising each morning,
must therefore bask in the mellow light,
the little light-reflecting clouds, little deer,
kind offices that don't offend. Clear rules:
that all things be horizontal,
the curves smooth and bound by time,
the holes and caves plugged with gravel,
matter absolutely predictable,
even the motions of the heart distinct.
Then I recognize, I recognize,
I secretly dig, I pick through the topsoil
of our years of plastic, through a network
of arteries and veins. No, there's no way out.
At least on that we can agree. None.
Once there was that one guy
who sharpened knives with a stone
at the foot of the forest. His gray disc
shone as it spun, and the thin blade
caught and released the fading light
and might have been mistaken for a promise.
Another, a ferryman or shepherd
of souls, would read the veins on the leaves
in October or November. And the prophet
who barely spoke . . . Those voices
of hope rejected or re-rejected . . . All gone,
swallowed up or turned to stone.
And now, at the very end of autumn,
here it is, unbidden,
no flares or trumpets to herald its arrival,

con il suo volo di scatto e surplace,
ad accamparsi sul margine dello sconforto e della resa,
sopra fanghiglie reali e metaforiche,
leggera smeraldina la libellula
in sospensione sull'aria
e quasi immota nel frusciare imperscrutabile
delle sue quattro ali di garza iridescente,
intarsiate. Scoccata
come un'analogia dall'arco teso
di un'immagine o intuizione subitanea
e in un lampo già altrove, su uno stelo
o un canneto, metamorfosi
in corso o indecifrabile
annuncio di qualcosa, messaggera
dei cieli e degli stagni,
qui e là, sopra e sotto, davanti,
sempre, davanti
o tutt'intorno a noi,
a negare l'ovvio a schiudere
un'altra più segreta geometria.

with its fitful flight, decamped
on the edge of discomfort and surrender,
over the real and metaphorical muck,
weightless emerald dragonfly
held in the air
by the inscrutable almost motionless rustle
of its four gauzy, iridescent, tessellated
wings. Shot
like an analogy from the stretched bow
of an image or sudden intuition
and in a flash already elsewhere, on a stalk
or the tip of a reed, ongoing
metamorphosis or indecipherable
annunciation of something, messenger
sent from heaven and the ponds,
here and there, above and below, ahead,
always ahead of
or all around us,
denying the obvious to reveal
another more hidden pattern.

3

"Ehi capo" mi chiede un ragazzotto dietro l'angolo,
ritto accanto a uno scooter stercorario,
che sulla non immensa
fronte indossa un diadema piumato,
Toro Seduto o Geronimo,
"posso rubarle un minutino, solo per due questioni?
È una ricerca di mercato!" E prima di ascoltare
la eventuale risposta o il diniego
giù s'attuffa, sventaglia
ilare il suo bel mitra di domande:
cosa penso cioè se penso qualcosa del problema
dei troppi asilanti stranieri delinquenti, se credo
anch'io che sia ora di fare un bel repulisti,
un bel muro per tutti questi negri e questi mongoli,
qualcosa di concreto insomma, se leggo "Il mattino
della domenica" regolarmente ogni domenica appunto
oppure solo quando mi capita
e dove (al bar, a casa, allo stadio),
o me ne frego. E quando provo a dire
che io sono uno che se legge preferisce
al nerofumo mattutino "La sera del dì di festa"
o anche le nebbie vaghe
che salgono in certe albe sopra i prati e sui fiumi,
irrompe il Va' pensiero
del suo cellulare, lui ascolta, sgrana gli occhi
e "Merda!" fa "devo schizzare, grazie
mister" e va, sventoloso di piume,
vespa del fango che cavalca un dromedario,
per qualche territorio di nequizia o conquista,

3

"Yo chief," calls a kid around the corner,
propped against his beetle-shaped scooter.
On his narrow crown
he wears a crown of feathers,
like Sitting Bull or Geronimo.
"We're doing a survey,
you got a minute?" Before I have time
to answer or wave him away
he plunges ahead and happily
unloads his barrage of questions:
What do I think, that is, if I think anything,
about all these foreign criminals seeking asylum?
Do I agree it's time we clean house,
build a beautiful wall for these Blacks and mongoloids?
Take, you know, concrete action? Do I read
the local Lega paper regularly like every Sunday
or only when I come across a copy?
And where is that (the café, the stadium, home)?
Or don't I care? And when I try to tell him
I'm the kind of person who prefers to read
on coal black mornings "The Evening of the Holiday"
or else the vague mists
rising off the fields and rivers at the start of some days
his ringtone, "*Va' pensiero,*"
erupts. He listens, his eyes get wide.
"Shit!" he says, "Gotta run, thanks,
mister," and off he goes, feathers fluttering,
a muddy wasp mounting a camel,
headed for some den of iniquity or land of conquest.

qui si riaccende il silenzio e la straducola
scende di nuovo al lago,
quasi mesta. Si disintegra
il paesaggio in migliaia di particelle
di rimorsi e di luce, di assenze. Il vuoto è vuoto,
il pieno non è pieno di niente,
o sono cose che paiono adesso insulse e che non placano
il morso della nuova afasia. La cavità
del lago è una voragine
priva di fondo e spessore, superficie
uguale, sovrapposta a se stessa, scolorita:
manca tutto. E in questo nulla si respira e s'implode,
e questo forse è il male, il vero male
senza rimedio o remissione, senza gloria,
l'occhio glauco del ritmo rassegnato,
lo spazio troppo angusto, soffocante
in cui nessuno abita davvero
e tutti sopravvivono a se stessi
non privi di malizia.
                    (No. No cari,
questa non è soltanto una faccenda privata.)

The wick of silence is relit, and the dirt road
descends once more to the lake,
morose-like. The landscape
breaks up into a thousand particles:
regret, light, absence. The emptiness is empty,
the fullness full of nothing,
or things appear dull and won't mitigate
the sting of this new speechlessness. The cratered
lake is a whirlpool
with no bottom or depth, its surface
uniform, overlapping, colorless—
all's gone. In this nothingness you breathe and implode.
So this is evil, perhaps, real evil,
irredeemable and unremitting, no glory,
the glaucous eye of a dying beat,
a suffocatingly cramped space
inhabited by none,
where everyone fends for himself
and no one's innocent.
                        (No. No, dears,
this isn't some private matter.)

4

Vortica, poi scompare. Subitanea
riemerge sopra il verde,
resta immobile,
sospesa a trasparenze e forse spia
minuscole prede nell'acqua,
da cui viene. Fuoriuscita
dall'acqua in una vita precedente, ora signora
dell'aria e del volo.

       (Cosa fanno
di notte, le libellule? Dormono?
E dove dormono, e che sogni
traversano i loro minimi
cieli notturni in brevissimi
fremiti del corpo o della coda?)

       Un equilibrio
miracoloso: proprio questo. Una musica
che appare solo a istanti, per vettori
e frattali,
zig zag.

       (La libellula
ha un'età rispettabile: ne esistevano
di enormi, dentro il cupo delle ere
antichissime. Chissà quanto aggraziate:
libellule così lunghe e veloci,
chissà come volavano
attorno ai colli tozzi

4

It twirls and disappears. Suddenly
reemerges above the greenery,
hovers
on transparent wings, and seems to spy
tiny prey in the water
from which it came. Sprung
from water in a past life, now a lady
piloting the air.

               (What do they do
at night? Do they sleep?
Where do they sleep? What dreams
traverse their narrow
night skies and make
body and tail briefly tremble?)

                   Miraculous
balance: that's it. A music
that comes in fits, vectors
and fractals,
zigzag.

                  (The dragonfly
has a distinguished age: there used to be
giant ones in the dark eras
of the ancient past. What graceful shapes
they must have taken:
dragonflies long and fast
floating about
the beefy necks of dinosaurs,

dei dinosauri, sotto gli occhi
vacui di pterodattili e carnivori
tiranni.

                           E chissà
che feste a risalire le sequoie verso la vampa
dei soli e dei pianeti, un turbinìo
dattilico di gioia. Le danzatrici
dell'aria: possiamo dire così?)
Ma loro, poi,
nel battito improvviso delle ali,
cosa vogliono dirci? Cosa possono
dirci, le libellule?
Cosa ancora?

under the vacant
stares of pterodactyls and meat-eating
tyrants.

                    And what bliss
it must be to climb sequoias into the flash
of suns and planets, a whirl of
dactylic joy! Airborne
dancers—can we call them that?)
But what is it
with their sudden wingbeats
they mean to tell us? What can they
tell us, dragonflies?
What more?

5

Ecco il giorno degli uomini fermi,
degli sguardi perduti.

Il primo, che sta fisso
sul terrapieno della ferrovia, segue gli snodi
con gli occhi, dei binari, come segmenti
di un caos inestricabile; un altro è immobile
di fronte a una fontana che singhiozza.
L'acqua sembra pulsare
ritmicamente, ma è una fatica il ritmo, un grumo
rumoroso che raspa nella gola. Passa un treno,
scompare. Scatta un segnale, uno scambio,
scende il fiotto, e il po' d'acqua che strapiomba
si mescola con l'acqua che ristagna, si fa uguale
e invisibile nel tutto.

Ai margini, sbilenchi
sulla scarpata, gli arbusti:
tagliati netti al piede, come nude cicatrici
su un terreno che diresti inospitale,
e anche questo sarebbe un errore.
Dura e fredda, la terra li accoglie
e cresceranno in bosco
e fulgore.

La durata
e l'istante irripetibile, l'immagine
che passa e trascorre in un flusso,
il continuo e il discreto: è questo il punto? L'esistenza
scomposta e ricomposta, che si allarga

5

These are the days of idle men,
blank looks.

The first is frozen
beside the railway, riveted by the twisting tracks,
as if they were segments of a chaos
he can't make sense of. Another stands
facing a fountain that pumps in fits and starts.
The water seems to move
to a rhythm, but its rhythm is strained, a clot
rasping in the throat. A train passes
and disappears. A signal goes off, a switch,
down comes the jet in dribs and drabs
that mix with the standing water until it's all one
invisible body of water.

On the periphery, shrubs
kink to one side of the escarpment:
sheared at the bottom, like exposed scars
on ground that you'd call barren.
You'd be wrong about that too.
The cold hard land hugs them
and they'll grow into forest
and refulgence.

The time it lasts
and the fleeting moment, the image
that ebbs and flows,
the continuous and discrete—is that the point? Existence
made and unmade, enlarged

o si torce in dolore o che procede
di sé e delle altrui vite disattenta,
come stasi insensata?
Quando non vedi non senti
non ti accorgi non provi
curiosità o emozioni: un ronzio,
forse, inaudibile, accompagna
la tua vacanza, il vuoto, e quelle fasi
o tappe del circuito
elettrico del mondo in cui cammini.

Il tizio
ai piedi di un pannello luminoso, le lucine
che minime baluginano azzurre
e poco dopo rosee, e dopo azzurre:
singole trafitture, si domanda,
o macchia indefinibile? Una libellula, forse,
interiore apre e chiude la mente,
svola nel nervo ottico, percorre
i lunghi corridoi della memoria, discontinua
guizza attraverso le forme e le immagini, i volti,
i nomi delle cose, le parole . . .

or writhing in pain or going along
indifferent to itself and others,
like mindless stasis?
When you don't see don't hear
take no notice feel neither
intrigued nor moved: a buzzing
maybe, barely audible, accompanies
your holiday, the emptiness, and those points
or stops along the electric
circuit of the world you walk in.

Somebody
underneath a railway signal, the lights
barely flashing blue
and shortly after pink, and after blue—
is each a wound, or are they
illegible stains? Like a dragonfly,
the inner mind opens and closes,
flies about the optic nerve, travels
the long corridors of memory, intermittently
darts from form to image to face
to the names of things, to words . . .

6

Non proprio una damigella, no davvero.
Piuttosto una signora che ha qualcosa
di meno prevedibile, come una pratica lunga
di speranze deluse e tentativi.
Libellula depressa, si può dire. Valli e valli
da risalire o scendere, pianure
cosparse di detriti. Un petalo,
diciamo, trascinato
da venti strepitosi in un deserto.
Un petalo o un fiore
che ricordino tutto nell'esilio: alberi, api
e quelle ali nell'aria
quei profumi ancora possibili sperabili
persino nell'asfalto.
In un deserto d'asfalto o sul verde di un lago:
nella memoria dell'acqua
chiusa che pensa al mare. Qui,
cosa ti ha condotto? Impossibile,
impossibile ricostruire ogni cosa, lo sai.
Inutile custodire, forse. Vago
anche ogni eventuale residuo progetto,
solo questo
dono barbarico: un'arida,
dimessa collana di api morte
diceva il poeta. Non molto,
d'accordo. Ma resta
ancora una cosa che accende
di nuovo rosso la strada, per un attimo,

6

No damsel. Not by a long shot.
More like a woman with something
harder to detect, like long practice
in dashed hopes and efforts.
Call her a depressed dragonfly. Valley after valley
to climb or descend, plains
littered with debris. A petal,
say, dragged
across a desert on blasts of wind.
A petal or a flower
reminiscent of all exiles: trees, bees
and those wings in the air,
those smells that we can still hope for
even on blacktop.
In a desert of blacktop or on the green scrim of a lake.
In the memory of landlocked water
that makes one think of the sea.
What led you here? You know
it's impossible to reconstruct everything. Impossible.
Maybe pointless to protect. And any
plans for the future are unclear.
Nothing but this
wild gift: a plain
dry necklace of dead bees,
says the poet. Not much,
agreed. Still,
something remains to turn
the road momentarily red again

e conduce
comunque un po' più avanti.

Un'ultima cosa. Vamos a ver.

Nella quiete
provvisoria del volo, lo smeraldo
che pulsa e riflette
l'ultima povera luce del giorno,
quasi distribuendo
agli occhi che hanno voglia di guardare
un obolo di sole un po' di forza,
stremata estenuata la libellula
forse dice soltanto el compartir
es la ley del camino, non altro.

Spezza il pane, dividilo.

Prima di intrufolarsi nella notte
che viene e dentro cui
prosegue, come noi che la seguiamo
a distanza nel dubbio
nella musica incerta
che ci accomuna forse
e ci fa uguali. Quasi uguali
e diversi. Vamos,
vamos a ver.

Un'ultimissima cosa.

and leads us
a little farther on.

                One last thing. Vamos a ver.

Its flight
briefly suspended, its emerald
pulses and reflects
the last weak light of day,
almost filling
your searching eyes
with an obol of sun, a little force,
all the exhausted dragonfly
may have to say is el compartir
es la ley del camino. Nothing more.

                Break bread, share it.

Before it slips into the night
coming on and in which
it travels, like us, following after it
at a distance, doubting
the uncertain music
that may bind us together
and make us equals. Almost equals
and different. Vamos,
vamos a ver.

                One more one last thing.

Acknowledgments

Poems in this collection have been selected from *Le cose senza storia* (Marcos y Marcos, 1994), *Pietra sangue* (Marcos y Marcos, 1999), *Folla sommersa* (Marcos y Marcos, 2004), *Corpo stellare* (Marcos y Marcos, 2011), *Argéman* (Marcos y Marcos, 2014), and *Cenere, o terra* (Marcos y Marcos, 2018). The original Italian versions are reproduced with kind permission of the publisher.

Thank you to the editors of the journals in which some of these translations have appeared: *The Arkansas International*, *Bitter Oleander*, *Mid-American Review*, *Sewanee Review*, and *Waxwing*. "History of Language" was reprinted by *Poetry Daily*.

Completion of the translations was made possible by a Raiziss/de Palchi Translation Award from the Academy of American Poets. Thanks to the judges.

My deep gratitude to Peter Cole, Richard Sieburth, and Rosanna Warren; to Michael Collier and Michael F. Moore; to my colleagues at Goucher College, particularly Phaye Poliakoff-Chen, Elizabeth Spires, and Madison Smartt Bell.

Author's Notes

Irrigation Channel: *Parisiennes* are a popular brand of cigarettes in Switzerland. There are various labels; this poem refers to the red label.

Witness: The poem is based on a true story. The protagonist is my father.

Palace Beach: The events in this poem are also true, or close to the truth, though the man mistaken for a German officer turned out to be an elderly retiree from a town in Upper Ticino who was there on vacation.

Night Visit: Cratoids, Armpullers, and Sneeze the Dragon are figments of my daughter Nina's imagination. Anna Brichtova (February 24, 1930–May 15, 1944) was one of the children transported to the concentration camp in Theresienstadt, outside Prague. All that remains of her is a drawing, now on display at the museum near the Jewish Cemetery.

Pietra Sangue: The term refers to scagliola, or "poor man's marble." According to information collected in the province of Como, the chalk and glue stone (generally black with stylized inlays and drawings in various colors) was polished with seven rare hematite stones. The last is called, in dialect, *pietra saanch*. Apparently working with these stones is a delicate operation, for hematite is said to *tira fö 'l bèl e la làsa lì 'l brut*—bring out the beautiful but leave behind the ugly.

Buried Crowd: In September 2001 Paul Hooghe, then 102 years old, died in Brussels. According to newspapers at the time, he was the last surviving veteran of the Great War. In 1916 he was drafted into the Fifth Regiment of Lancers and transferred to the grenadiers just before the armistice. I am indebted to the historian Gigi Corazzol's reflections in *La palla di Farra di Mel. Un viaggio in altalena* (Terraferma, 2002) on the length of collective memory in human civilizations and the so-called floating gap.

Testimonies: The poem is about a homicide that occurred years ago in a government-subsidized building in Chiasso, where my mother lived.

Two Herons: The last lines in section 1 allude to the name originally given to the American war in Afghanistan (Infinite Justice), later abandoned for fear of offending Islam and replaced with the equally obscene Enduring Peace. Lagh Doss is a tiny body of water near the village of San Bernardino, in Switzerland. The heron in section 2 passes there very early in the morning every summer. One time, in the Soldo Valley, I managed to sneak up on it and follow its flight.

Ghosts at a Terry Blue Concert: The concert was held in the Palapenz warehouse in Chiasso. Terry Blue is my son Leo's stage name.

History of Language: Echoes of the war and the demise of Benito Mussolini and Claretta Petacci could be heard in children's games well into the 1950s.

Climbing to Cristallina: From a song by Emerson, Lake & Palmer on the album *Pictures at an Exhibition*, a rock adaptation of Modest Mussorgsky's suite. The Cristallina is a lodge in Upper Ticino, below the summit of the same name.

Calcite Stars: The stars and subterranean scene are inspired by the Castellana Caves in the Salento, in southern Italy. The master/friend is Philippe Jaccottet.

Dragonfly: In section 3, the local paper alluded to is *Il mattino della domenica*, a tasteless and dangerous weekly put out by the Ticino League (Lega dei Ticinesi), a political party that is arguably crasser than Italy's Northern League Party. In section 6, the quoted lines are Osip Mandelstam's. The Spanish phrases are taken from Cormac McCarthy's novel *Cities of the Plain*. It was not until after writing the poem that I thought of Amelia Rosselli's *Dragonfly* (Libellula).

The Complete Elegies of Sextus Propertius, translated with introduction and notes by Vincent Katz

Knowing the East, by Paul Claudel, translated with introduction and notes by James Lawler

Enough to Say It's Far: Selected Poems of Pak Chaesam, translated by David R. McCann and Jiwon Shin

In Hora Mortis/Under the Iron of the Moon: Poems, by Thomas Bernhard, translated by James Reidel

The Greener Meadow: Selected Poems, by Luciano Erba, translated by Peter Robinson

The Dream of the Poem: Hebrew Poetry from Muslim and Christian Spain, 950–1492, translated, edited, and introduced by Peter Cole

The Collected Lyric Poems of Luís de Camões, translated by Landeg White

C. P. Cavafy: Collected Poems, Bilingual Edition, translated by Edmund Keeley and Philip Sherrard, edited by George Savidis, with a new preface by Robert Pinsky

Poems Under Saturn: Poèmes saturniens, by Paul Verlaine, translated and with an introduction by Karl Kirchwey

Final Matters: Selected Poems, 2004–2010, by Szilárd Borbély, translated by Ottilie Mulzet

Selected Poems of Giovanni Pascoli, translated by Taije Silverman with Marina Della Putta Johnston

After Callimachus: Poems, by Stephanie Burt, with a foreword by Mark Payne

Dear Ms. Schubert: Poems by Ewa Lipska, translated by Robin Davidson and Ewa Elżbieta Nowakowska, with a foreword by Adam Zagajewski

The Translator of Desires, by Muhyiddin Ibn 'Arabi, translated by Michael Sells

Cantigas: Galician-Portuguese Troubadour Poems, translated and introduced by Richard Zenith

The Owl and the Nightingale: A New Verse Translation, translated
   by Simon Armitage

Brief Homage to Pluto and Other Poems, by Fabio Pusterla, selected
   and translated by Will Schutt

† Out of print